The Whole World Is A
Single Flower

The Whole World Is A Single Flower

365 Kong-ans for Everyday Life

with questions and commentary by

Zen Master Seung Sahn

and a foreword by Stephen Mitchell

Edited by Jane McLaughlin, JDPSN and Paul Muenzen

Charles E. Tuttle Company, Inc.
Boston • Rutland, Vermont • Tokyo

Published by the Charles E. Tuttle Company, Inc.
of Rutland, Vermont & Tokyo, Japan
with editorial offices at 77 Central Street, Boston, Massachusetts
02109.

BQ
9289.5
.S48
1992

Library of Congress Cataloging-in-Publication Data
Seung Sahn.
    The whole world is a single flower :
    365 kong-ans for everyday life /
    Seung Sahn ; with a foreword by Stephen Mitchell ;
    edited by Jane McLaughlin and Paul Muenzen.
      p. cm.
    Includes index.
    ISBN 0-8048-1782-0 (alk. paper) :
    1. Koan. 2. Zen meditations. I. Title,
BQ9289.5.S48 1992   91-67336
294.3'443—dc20   CIP

Permissions and Acknowledgments
"The Story of Seung Sahn Soen-sa," by Stephen Mitchell, reprinted from
Dropping Ashes on the Buddha, The Teaching of Zen Master Seung Sahn, ©
1976 by The Providence Zen Center, Inc., compiled and edited by Stephen
Mitchell, is reprinted by permission of Grove Weidenfeld.

Selections from Lao-Tzu, © 1988 by Stephen Mitchell, reprinted from *Tao Te
Ching*, A New English Version by Stephen Mitchell, by permission of Harper
Collins Publishers and Macmillan London Ltd. First lines of selections from
the *Tao Te Ching* used in *The Whole World Is A Single Flower*: "The Tao that can
be told", "Therefore the Master", "The Master leads by emptying people's
minds", "The Tao doesn't take sides", "The Tao is called the Great Mother",
"The Tao is infinite, eternal", "The supreme good is like water", "Do your
work, then step back", "Giving birth and nourishing", "Colors blind the eye",
"See the world as your self", "Look, and it can't be seen", "Empty your mind
of all thoughts", "When the Master governs, the people", "When the great
Tao is forgotten", "Throw away holiness and wisdom", "The Master keeps
her mind always at one with the Tao", "The Master, by residing in the Tao",
"If you open yourself to the Tao", "If you want to accord with the Tao",
"There was something formless and perfect", "Thus the Master is available to
all people", "There is a time for being ahead", "The Tao can't be perceived",
"The great Tao flows everywhere", "The Tao never does anything."

Calligraphy: frontispiece "Kwan Um" (Perceive World Sound) by Zen Master
Seung Sahn; p. vi calligraphy by Hakuyu Taizan Maezumi, Roshi; p. xxii
"Only Don't Know" by Jakusho Kwong, Roshi, Sonoma Mt. Zen Center; p.
226 "Go Straight" by Zen Master Seung Sahn; p. 237 "Mu Mu Mu" by Zen
Master Seung Sahn.

First Printing
PRINTED IN THE UNITED STATES

Contents

Foreword

Many years ago, when Dae Soen Sa Nim first came to America, he was called simply Soen Sa Nim ("Honorable Zen Master"). He was just as great a teacher back then. The Dae ("Great") was added as a sixtieth birthday present, as is the tradition in Korea. Maybe after he is seventy he will be called Dae Dae Soen Sa Nim. Things have a tendency to expand around him.

There used to be 10 gates. Now he has put together a collection of 365 kong-ans. I look forward to future kong-an books he may be preparing, which will celebrate the 8,760 hours of the year, then the 525,600 minutes, and finally the 31,536,000 seconds. If he goes on from there to collect a kong-an for each of the nano-seconds, I'm afraid that all the trees in the galaxy won't be sufficient to make a single copy of that book. Not that this would stop him.

One of the distinctive qualities of *The Whole World Is a Single Flower* is its ecumenism. Dae Soen Sa Nim has included not only kong-ans from Chinese and Korean Zen, but also from Lao-tzu and the Christian tradition. The connection between Buddhism and the founding teachers of Taoism is well known:

> China was prepared for Buddhism by the teachings of the I Ching (incorporated in Taoism), which emphasize compassion and self-reliance, egolessness and enlightenment, service for the good of all, deeds without selfish profit, non-violence and tranquillity, and the recognition of eternal change, or transformation. All these elements are clearly explained in Lao-tzu's Tao Te Ching, which expressed the Bodhisattva ideal of the Mahayana more than five hundred years before the introduction of Buddhism in China.
>
> (Lama Govinda, *The Inner Structure of the I Ching*)

The old Masters themselves acknowledged and honored this kinship. Here is Zen Master Hsueh-tou (980-1052), compiler of the famous kong-an collection *The Blue Cliff Record*:

> The moon floats above the pine trees
> as you sit on the veranda in the cool evening air.
> Your fingertips move lightly along the flute.
> The melody is so lovely that it makes the listeners weep.
> But Zen's flute has no holes
> and its ancient, clear music is beyond emotion.
> Don't even try to play it
> unless you can make the Great Sound of Lao-tzu.

Dae Soen Sa Nim is, as far as I know, the first Zen Master whose collection includes kong-ans taken from a Christian author. In this he is showing the open-mindedness and adaptability that have always characterized his teaching, from his early days in America in 1972-73, when his young hippie students, with their acid trips and casual nudity, must have seemed to him like creatures from another planet: fascinating, barbaric, full of potential. Like all keen-eyed Zen Masters, he is using what is available, in the community and in the culture.

> The Master is available to all people
> and doesn't reject anyone.
> He is ready to use all situations
> and doesn't waste anything.
> This is called embodying the light.
>   (Tao Te Ching, chapter 27)

Religions are languages to express what is beyond language. In the beginning was the Word, but before the beginning there was not even a whisper. When the Buddha held up a flower, when Jesus took a child in his arms, they were saying the same thing. We can point to that thing with words from any religious language. So emptiness equals fullness, and the kingdom of God equals the Bodhisattva mind. (As a postscript, I would like to add one Jewish kong-an: *The Bible says that God's true name is "I am." What is this "I am"?*)

Dae Soen Sa Nim has asked me to say something about kong-ans and the Tao. I would like to make two points.

The first is that all the answers are already inside us. We don't need to look anywhere else.

This proposition has a corollary: When anything is wrong in our lives, we should look inside ourselves for the karmic hindrance. "If you blame someone else," the Sixth Patriarch said, "you yourself are to blame. If you think you are a victim, it is that very thought which makes you a victim." Confucius said, "In the archer there is a resemblance to the mature person. When he misses the bull's-eye, he turns and seeks the reason for his failure in himself."

The second point is that all our understanding is useless if we want to truly understand. "Don't be *too* intelligent," Dae Soen Sa Nim used to say. "It's like hitting a golf ball with a putter: when you hit the ball too hard, it jumps out of the cup, even if your aim is perfect." The best way to enter the vivid current of the Tao is to let go of everything we think we know. The simplest mind is the best.

If kong-ans are questions that we work on only in the interview room or on our meditation cushions, they are of limited value. It is true that both ancient Masters and contemporary students have had experiences of deep insight through this work. But even more important, I think, kong-ans are good practice because they are practice for life. Working on them prepares us for the great natural kong-ans that life so rudely and compassionately presents us with: What must I do to completely let go of my mother and father, and thus become truly mature? How can I clarify my money karma and achieve right livelihood? What changes do I have to make in myself so that my marriage can become a radiant transmission of the Dharma? These natural kong-ans may take years, decades, of excruciating work.

Kong-an practice teaches us to wait under the cloud of unknowing, looking where there is nothing to see, listening where there is nothing to hear. Eventually we understand that all solutions come to us by themselves, from the well of being, if only we stop trying to control. The secret is trust. When we trust ourselves to not-know, we learn how to trust the radiant creativity of the Tao, the intelligence of the universe.

Do you have the patience to wait
till your mud settles and the water is clear?
Can you remain unmoving
till the right action arises by itself?

The Master doesn't seek fulfillment.
Not seeking, not expecting,
  she is present, and can welcome all things.
    (Tao Te Ching, chapter 15)

Each of Dae Soen Sa Nim's 365 kong-ans is important, and each question that a good teacher holds up to your face like a mirror.

But there is one essential kong-an: the 366th: the kong-an that is our life. When we resolve it, every year is leap year.

STEPHEN MITCHELL

Editors' Preface

It is said by many that the first transmission of Zen occurred when Shakyamuni Buddha held up a single flower before an assembly of his followers. No one in the vast gathering at Vulture's Peak could comprehend what their teacher was trying to say. Only Mahakashyapa smiled. This smile would cause the Buddha to say, "I transmit my true Dharma to you." And so began the lineage and teaching of Zen, the mind-to-mind transmission which continues to this day. Throughout years of change and adaptation as it spread from culture to culture, Zen teaching has always returned to this upraised flower, or whatever else points directly to truth: *"What is this?"* This basic enquiry into the nature of things is the place where Zen practice is born, and it is the function of kong-an practice [J: *koan*, Ch: *kung-an*] to deepen and direct this enquiry, what is often called the Great Question.

This collection of three hundred and sixty-five kong-ans is the work of a contemporary Zen Master who has lived in and taught throughout the West for over twenty years. It is the fruit of his lifelong efforts to bring traditional Zen practice to students who are otherwise unfamiliar with its centuries-old methods. Zen Master Seung Sahn is the 78th Patriarch in a lineage of succession reaching back to Shakyamuni Buddha, and since receiving, at the age of 22, the only Dharma Transmission that Zen Master Ko Bong ever gave, he has been spending time between his native Korea and wherever in the East or West throughout the world his students ask him to teach.

This book marks the first time that a prominent Zen Master has published a collection of traditional Buddhist kong-ans including kong-ans specifically derived from Christian and Taoist sources. As such, it is a significant milestone in the growing dialogue between Buddhism and Christianity, especially as Buddhism becomes a more established tradition in the West, and as Christians increasingly search for ways to use some of the meditative forms and practices of the East to deepen their rich tradition of comtemplative prayer.

The Christian kong-ans, which begin with kong-an 62, are derived from poems written by the German mystic and poet Johannes Scheffler (1624-1677), known to the world as Angelus Silesius, the Wandering Cherub. For several years, Zen Master Seung Sahn has been leading retreats for Catholic Cistercian monks at the Abbey of Gethsemani in Kentucky, where Thomas Merton had lived and conducted his dialogue with the religious traditions of the East. The Silesius poems were shown to Zen Master Seung Sahn by some of the monks there, among them Br. Benjamin and Br. Anthony, and, since the monks at Gethsemani had been using them as touchstones for contemplative prayer, he turned them into kong-ans during the Gethsemani retreats. Now these monks use Zen kong-an practice in the context of prayer and reflection. Willigis Jager translated the poems from the German original. They are exquisite renderings and we are very grateful to have them.

The Taoist kong-ans are based on Stephen Mitchell's widely acclaimed 1988 translation of the *Tao Te Ching*. In addition to granting us permission to reprint these translations, Mr. Mitchell has contributed a Foreword and has allowed us to reprint his short biography from Zen Master Seung Sahn's first book, *Dropping Ashes on the Buddha* (Grove Weidenfeld, 1976), which Mr. Mitchell compiled and edited.

The "traditional" Zen kong-ans have been brought together from several sources. Chief among these sources is Zen Master Seung Sahn's own tradition as a monk in the Chogye Order in Korea. Many of the Korean kong-ans contained in this book have not been recorded in any systematic way. These stories, observations, and dialogues of famous (and obscure) Korean Masters are often preserved almost exclusively in the memory of those students who happened to witness the original incidents and settings which gave rise to spontaneous teaching. They also represent the teaching of Zen Master Seung Sahn's dharma "family," especially Zen Master Man Gong and Zen Master Ko Bong, two of the greatest Masters of their time. It is our sincere hope that this collection preserves at least some part of our vital link to this irreplaceable oral tradition.

Another source has been the *Gateless Gate* [*Mumon Kwan*] and the *Blue Cliff Record* [Ch: *Pi-Yen-Nu*; J: *Hekigan Roku*], two traditional kong-an collections used by Zen Masters in Japan and Korea from the thirteenth century onwards. The selections used here are Zen Master Seung Sahn's own translations from the Chinese, to which he has added the questions and commentary. People who are familiar with previously published editions of the *Mumon Kwan* and *Blue Cliff Record* will note a difference in spelling used in the translations here presented. This is merely the Korean transliteration of the Chinese original, which Zen Master Seung Sahn pronounces and which his students have learned from him over the years: the Chinese Master Chao-chou [J: Joshu] is spelled Joju throughout the text, and the T'ang dynasty Master Yun Men [J: Ummon] is spelled Un Mun. Regarding the transliteration from Korean, there is even less science. The determination of spelling is always tricky. While there are certain well-known transliteration systems available, we have chosen spellings more from the standpoint of usage and practice. In addition, many of these kong-ans were gathered from talks, interviews, and private dialogues with Zen Master Seung Sahn, and were never translated from any specific texts or written sources. To readers familiar with the McCune-Reischauer or Wade-Giles systems, some of our spellings may be a little imprecise. These will be made more consistent in any future edition.

The author of this book is not a native English speaker. While making every attempt to bring this language into line with customary and everyday English, we have tried to preserve what is unique about Zen Master Seung Sahn's peculiar usage of the language. Phrases such as "only don't know," "together-action," and "enough-mind fish never touches the hook" reveal an economy of phrasing which it would be rather impossible to duplicate in some other form without ruining the utter simplicity and one-pointedness of the situation to which he is responding at any given moment. One of his students, who had studied Korean and Chinese characters for several years, said to the Zen Master, "Many Zen phrases and teaching terms are not translateable. It seems impossible to try to express it in the English language, which is so dry and logical." Zen Master Seung Sahn replied, "So, my style English appeared." We hope we have preserved this spontaneous quality in the text.

The cover calligraphy, "The whole world is a single flower," is the work of Zen Master Man Gong (1872-1946), the author's grandteacher. The calligraphy on page *vi* is by Taizan Maezumi, Roshi of Zen Center of Los Angeles. The calligraphy on page *xxii* was graciously offered by Jakusho Kwong, Roshi of the Sonoma Mountain Zen Center. Throughout the rest of the text, the calligraphies are the work of Zen Master Seung Sahn.

This book has been nothing if not collaborative. We want to express our special gratitude to Mu Deung, Ji Do Poep Sa Nim, who throughout the early stages of this book provided outstanding leadership and dedication to an often tedious project. His clear-sighted command of the teaching, as well as his long experience with and love for it, enabled him constantly to protect this collection from potentially damaging editorial intrusions and missteps.

Thanks are also due to Neil Bartholomew for his technical and editorial assistance during the initial stages.

We benefited much from the generosity and assistance of many individuals, among them Mu Ryang Sunim, Jacob Perl, JDPSN, Do An Sunim, JDPSN, Robert Genthner, JDPSN, Mu Sang Sunim, Merrie Fraser, Diana Lynch, Mu Soeng Sunim, Mu Shim Sunim, Richard Streitfeld, J.W. Harrington, George Bowman, JDPSN, Il Ah Sunim; and the 1991 residents and staff of the Cambridge Zen Center, individually, and chief among them the Abbot, Do Mun Sunim. Many special thanks are due to Mr. Min Yong Lee of Harvard University, and to Mr. Chang Nam Yoon of the Harvard-Yenching Library. We are also very grateful to everyone at Charles E. Tuttle Company for their hard work, outstanding professionalism, and respect for the nature of this book.

Finally, we thank the supporters and participants of the 1990-91 Shin Won Sah International Winter Kyol Che: Zen Master Boek Am Sunim, the dozens of devoted supporters from Hwa Gye Sah Temple in Seoul (especially Jong Su Sunim, Ju Ji Sunim), and the monks and nuns of the Chogye Order. It is impossible to thank them all enough.

The bulk of this project was begun deep in the hills of South Korea, on the side of Mt. Kye Ryong San ("The Chicken Dragon Mountain"), at Shin Won Sah Temple, while the Gulf War unfolded, wreaking ecological havoc on the earth. Perhaps as many as 180,000 humans - and untold other beings - perished in the short span it took for these three hundred and sixty-five kong-ans to become a book. Why did this happen? An eminent teacher once said, "If one mind is clear, the whole universe is clear; if one mind is not clear, the whole universe is not clear. Only human beings don't understand their true self, so they don't know their correct job." If we perceive our mind, we perceive the vast suffering in this world. Then our job becomes clear.

Thank you to Zen Master Seung Sahn, Dae Soen Sa Nim, for coming to the West, for this wonderful, pure, direct teaching, and for helping all human beings find their correct situation, correct relationship, and correct function, all three hundred sixty-five days a year of it.

Only go straight, don't know. Try try try for ten thousand years non-stop, get enlightenment, and save all beings from suffering.

JANE MCLAUGHLIN, JDPSN
PAUL MUENZEN
Cambridge, MA
Winter, 1991

Correspondence regarding kong-ans can be sent to Zen Master Seung Sahn's designated teachers, called Ji Do Poep Sa Nims ("Guide to the Way"), at:

Kwan Um School of Zen
528 Pound Road
Cumberland, RI 02864

Essay

Early afternoon had been spent moving furniture out of the sitting room, arranging cushions and rug, gathering the food, setting tables, generally preparing for Zen Master Seung Sahn's arrival with Bob Genthner from the Lexington Zen Center. Some of us were from the monastery, some from a group of nearby hermitesses, some from Tennessee, from Florida and even a friend of Dae Soen Sa Nim from Korea (via Canada)! The Zen Master has been coming to us for a few day's retreat now for five years, and each visit is a great combination of hard work, insight, challenge, and great fun.

Why? Why does he come? Why do we attend, sit long hours, struggle with kong-ans, keep silence? Why do we come back each year?

I asked Dae Soen Sa Nim, "Why do you come to the Abbey each year?" He said, "It is easier to come here than for you to go to my Zen Centers, since you monks cannot travel, right?"

"Yes."

"Then I come here!"

That was it, his utter simplicity. The sincere way he lives what he is. Simple and true, it is too rare.

Our hermitage as monks of the Abbey of Gethsemani, of the Cistercian Order in the Roman Catholic Church, is to live with this sincerity and simplicity. We have been trying to do just this since 1098, the founding year of the Order. It has only enhanced this heritage and deepened it in my own life to have had the opportunity to sit and receive the teaching of Dae Soen Sa Nim.

Walking with the Zen Master down the road from the retreat house toward the Abbey, I wondered if he found our monastic life familiar. With a beaming smile he said, "Oh, yes! Same as in Korean monasteries. Same routine - up at 3 a.m. to chant, reading scriptures, a little food, silence, work. Our heads are shaved, we wear robes, just the same way!"

In the fourth century there was a strong spiritual movement of men and women who went out into the Egyptian desert to practice their Christian faith in solitude. Their experiences and their wisdom have remained a vital part of our Western heritage in the form of sayings and reminiscences, sometimes not unlike old Zen stories, and these are still used in the instruction of monks and nuns:

> Abbot Mark once said to Abbot Arsenius, "It is good, is it not, to have nothing in your cell that just gives you pleasure? For example, once I knew a brother who had a little wildflower that came up in his cell, and he pulled it out by the roots."

> "Well," said Abbot Arsenius, "that is all right. But each man should act according to his own spiritual ways. And if one were not able to get along without the flower, he should plant it again." (*The Wisdom of the Desert*, Thomas Merton, p. 67)

Perhaps *The Whole World Is a Single Flower* is an example of this little wildflower which has sprung up in our "cell," the whole world. Can we get along without this little flower? Dae Soen Sa Nim first arrived at the Abbey of Gethsemani very much like this little something which sprouted up in that desert brother's cell, and in my own practice he has spread seeds which grow and blossom in often unexpected ways.

Dae Soen Sa Nim's joy, his energy, his direct teaching going to the heart of the matter, resonate in our Cistercian monastic tradition, and very much in the desert tradition. Getting up at 3 a. m. we chant the psalms in choir. Why do we do this? If you ask the Zen Master says, "Just sing. Just chant." There is no need to check the performance.

Dae Soen Sa Nim's teaching is not new teaching. Most likely the desert monk's flower was no new flower. The teaching has always been here, all around us, within us. How could it be otherwise? What other teaching could be taught? Hills rise west of this monastery. The ploughed earth is brown. Each day we chant, each day we work, prepare food, wash the floors, run our business. Jesus taught that giving up a cup of cold water to one who thirsts is our "job." That is very familiar teaching to students of Dae Soen Sa Nim. With death each of the monks at the Abbey is buried behind the curving back wall of our church. No wonder Dae Soen Sa Nim is at home whenever he comes to our Abbey.

The thirteenth century Sufi poet Jalaluddin Rumi wrote:

> When you are with everyone but me,
>   you're with no one.
> When you are with no one but me, you're with everyone.
>
> Instead of being so bound up *with* everyone, *be* everyone.
> When you become that many, you're nothing. Empty.
> (*We Are Three*, Coleman Barks, p. 15.)

Who is this "me"?
Thank you, Dae Soen Sa Nim.

BROTHER BENJAMIN
Abbey of Gethsemani
Trappist, KY
August, 1991

Introduction

Zen means understanding your true self. "What am I?" That is a very important question: What is the one pure and clear thing? If you find the one pure and clear thing, you will have freedom from life and death. How is it possible to attain freedom from life and death? First, it is necessary that your direction becomes clear; if your direction is clear, then your life is clear. Why do you practice Zen? Why do you eat every day? You must find that!

Put it all down - your opinion, your condition, and your situation. Moment to moment just do it. Then there's no subject, no object, no inside, no outside. Inside and outside already become one. Then your direction and my direction, your action and my action are the same. This is called the Great Bodhisattva Way.

When you put it all down, you can believe in your true self one hundred percent. Then your mind is clear like space, which is clear like a mirror: red comes, red; white comes, white. Someone is hungry, give them food. Someone is thirsty, give them a drink. Everything is reflected in this clear mirror. Then you can see, hear, smell, taste, touch, and think clearly. The sky is blue, the tree is green; salt is salty, sugar is sweet. A dog is barking, "Woof! Woof!" Just like this, everything is truth. So you are also truth.

Then how does this truth function correctly? How do you make your life correct? Moment to moment, you must perceive your correct situation, correct relationship, and correct function. When you are hungry, what? If someone else is hungry, what? If you meet the Buddha, what do you do? Where do you throw away your cigarette ashes? Most people understand all of this, but they cannot actually *do* it. If you completely do it, then your everyday mind is correct life. Jesus said, "I am the Way, the Truth, and the Life." That is the same point.

Most people understand too much. This understanding cannot help your life. Descartes said, "I think, therefore I am." So "I" makes "I". If you are not thinking, then what? Even if you have a big experience, if you cannot attain the one pure and clear thing, then all your understanding and experience cannot help your practice. Therefore Zen practice is not about understanding. Zen means only go straight, don't know.

Joju once asked Master Nam Cheon, "What is the true way?"

Nam Cheon replied, "Everyday mind is the true way."

"Then should I try to keep it or not?"

Nam Cheon said, "If you try to keep it, you are already mistaken."

"If I do not try to keep it, how can I understand the true way?"

Nam Cheon replied, "The true way is not dependent on understanding or not understanding. Understanding is illusion; not understanding is blankness. If you completely attain the true way of not thinking, it is like space, clear and void. So why do you make right and wrong?" Joju heard that, and got enlightenment.

What did Joju attain?

Often, Zen students want to "keep it". That is a big mistake. Zen means when you are doing something, just do it. You already know that understanding is illusion. Don't be attached to your understanding! Correct practice means "How does your understanding get digested and become wisdom?" That is true everyday mind.

So why make 365 kong-ans? Since everybody understands too much, we must use understanding medicine. What did Joju attain? If you open your mouth, it's already a mistake! But if you are not thinking, the answer is pure and clear, always in front of you. Then how does your true "I" function correctly and save all beings?

The Tao is called the Great Mother:
empty yet inexhaustible,
it gives birth to infinite worlds.

It is always present within you.
You can use it any way you want.

How does the Tao give birth to infinite worlds? This is the same question, the same point.

In this collection there are Buddhist kong-ans, Christian kong-ans, Taoist kong-ans, and Zen kong-ans. There are old kong-ans and new kong-ans, but they are all the same: these beautiful words all teach correct direction. If you are attached to beautiful speech or holding your opinion, you cannot attain their true meaning. So put it all down – your opinion, your condition, and your situation. Then your mind is clear like space. Then a correct answer to any kong-an will appear by itself. This is wisdom.

When you try a kong-an, if you don't attain it, don't worry! Don't be attached to the kong-an, and also, don't try to *understand* the kong-an. Only go straight, don't know: try, try, try for ten thousand years, nonstop. Then you attain the Way, the Truth, and the Life, which means from moment to moment keeping the correct situation, correct relationship, and correct function. That is already Great Love, Great Compassion, and the Great Bodhisattva Way.

Not dependent on words,
A special transmission outside the sutras,
Pointing directly to mind,
See your true nature, become Buddha.

If you wish to pass through this gate, do not give rise to thinking. The Buddha taught all the Dharmas in order to save all minds. When you do not keep any of these minds, then what use is there for Dharmas?

I hope every day you don't make any thing, just *do* it, from moment to moment, attain the 365 kong-ans, get enlightenment, and save all beings from suffering.

The high sky is always blue. Water always flows into the ocean.

ZEN MASTER SEUNG SAHN
Providence Zen Center
December, 1991

1. Sok Sahn's "Seven Go Straights"

A long time ago in China, there was a famous Zen Master named Sok Sahn who died without giving transmission. After his funeral ceremony, somebody had to give a formal Dharma speech, so many people asked the Head Monk. As he was about to begin speaking from the high rostrum, Sok Sahn's attendant, a fifteen-year-old boy named Ku Bong, came forward and said, "Our teacher always taught about the seven kinds of going straight:

1. Go straight, resting.
2. Go straight, put it all down.
3. Go straight, the cold, clear water of autumn.
4. Go straight, one mind for 10,000 years.
5. Go straight, cold ashes under a rotten log.
6. Go straight, incense burner in an old temple (very heavy, never moving).
7. Go straight, one line of incense smoke rising in the still air.

If you understand the true meaning of the seven kinds of going straight, then you can give the Dharma speech. If you don't, you cannot."

"One color, different function," the Head Monk replied.

"I cannot believe that."

"If you don't believe me, I'll show you." The Head Monk then lit a stick of incense, placed it in the burner, and quietly watched it burn down. Then he died.

Many people exclaimed, "Ah, this great monk has also died!"

But the attendant only patted the Head Monk's back slowly three times, saying, "Sitting, die. Standing, die. Either way, no hindrance. But Sok Sahn's seven go straights' true meaning cannot be gotten, even in a dream."

1. *What do Sok Sahn's seven go straights mean?*
2. *What did the Head Monk's death mean?*
3. *The attendant said, "Sitting, die. Standing, die. Either way, no hindrance. But Sok Sahn's seven go straights' true meaning cannot be gotten, even in a dream." What does this mean?*

COMMENTARY: Seven doors into the same room. Each door has a different style and function. If you are attached to style and function you cannot enter the room. Only go straight through, take seven steps. Then you can see your true master and say, "How are you today?" "Fine, and you?" "Very good, thank you." Do you understand that? If you do, then you can pass Sok Sahn's seven go straights.

2. *The Correct Way, Truth and Correct Life*

During a Dharma talk at the Lexington Zen Center, Zen Master Seung Sahn said to the assembly, "In the Bible, Jesus says, 'I am the Way, the Truth and the Life.' Zen also says that if you attain your true self, then you attain the correct way, truth and correct life."

"So what is the correct way?" a student asked Zen Master Seung Sahn.

"Why do you eat every day? Only for your body, because of personal desire? Only for you? That is the same as being an animal. On the other hand, if your eating is for all beings, then your life and direction are clear. The name for that is the correct way."

"Then what is truth?" the student asked.

"If you attain the true way, your mind is clear like space. Then when you see and hear clearly, everything is truth."

"What is correct life?" the student asked.

Zen Master Seung Sahn answered, "If you attain the truth, then you must correctly function as truth, by keeping correct situation, correct relationship, and correct function, moment to moment. The names for this are Great Love, Great Compassion or the Great Bodhisattva Way. That is correct life."

The student bowed and said, "Thank you very much."

1. *Why do you eat every day?*
2. *Why is the sky blue?*
3. *When does sugar become sweet?*
4. *The way, the truth and the life – are they the same or different?*

COMMENTARY: The student goes to school, the army serves the country, and the teacher works for all students. The dog is barking, "Woof, woof"; the rooster is crowing, "Cock-a-doodle-doo!" Each one understands its job. What is your job? You must keep your obligation to your parents and to your country. When you are hungry, just eat. When someone else is hungry, give them food. Then you attain the correct way, truth and correct life.

3. *Moving Mountain? Moving Boat?*

One afternoon, Zen Master Man Gong and several of his students took a boat ride to An Myon Do Island. On the way, he pointed to a mountain and asked his students, "Is the mountain moving or is the boat moving?"

Hae Am stepped forward and said, "Neither the mountain nor the boat is moving. Mind is moving."

"How can you prove that?" Man Gong asked, whereupon Hae Am picked up a handkerchief and waved it. "When did you get this idea?" the Zen Master asked.

1. *Is the mountain moving or is the boat moving?*
2. *Zen Master Man Gong asked Hae Am, "When did you get this idea?" If you had been there, how would you have answered?*
3. *No boat, no mountain. Then what?*

COMMENTARY: Mountain is boat, boat is mountain. No mountain, no boat. Mountain is mountain, boat is boat. How do you keep the correct situation, relationship, and function of mountain and boat?

The boat is crossing the ocean to An Myon Do Island. The ocean is blue, the mountain is also blue. But the ocean is the ocean, and the mountain is the mountain.

4. Why Do You Have Two Eyes?

During an interview at the Los Angeles Dharma Zen Center, Zen Master Seung Sahn said to a student, "Human beings have two eyes, two nostrils and two ears, but only one mouth." He then asked her:

1.   *Why do you have two eyes?*
2.   *Why do you have one mouth?*
3.   *Why do you have two ears?*

COMMENTARY: Originally, human beings have no eyes, no ears, no nose, no tongue, no body and no mind. Who made the six roots? You, God, Buddha – which one? No, no, no. Cause and effect are very clear. Everything comes from your karma. The British gentleman and Indian laborer hug and pat each other, "Nice to meet you again."

5. How Many Hairs Do You Have on Your Head?

Zen Master Seung Sahn said to the assembly at the Providence Zen Center, "Everyone has hair on their head. Some people have a lot of hair, some people have only a little. Some people have long hair, some people have short hair." Then he asked:

1. *How many hairs do you have on your head?*
2. *How long is your hair?*

COMMENTARY: The ocean is full of water, there are many clouds in the sky. On the mountain there are numberless trees, and on one head there are many hairs. So form is emptiness, and emptiness is form.

Can you count the hairs on your head? How many do you have? If you find the correct answer then you clearly understand your job.

6. *This World Is Complete Stillness*

The Lotus Sutra says that all dharmas come from complete stillness. If you just go straight practicing, you have already arrived at Buddha's Hall.

1. *This world is already complete stillness. Then where do the sun, moon and stars come from?*
2. *What does "just go straight practicing" mean?*
3. *What is Buddha's Hall?*

COMMENTARY: The Bible says God made everything. Buddhism says mind made everything. Philosophers say consciousness made everything. A sutra says everything comes from emptiness. Which one is correct?

If you are not thinking, there is no name and form. Who made this world of name and form? Do you know? If you don't understand, go drink milk. Then this milk will teach you.

7. *Sumi Mountain*

One day, a monk asked Zen Master Un Mun, "Without thinking, is there a mistake or not?"
"Sumi Mountain," Un Mun replied.

"Already it's without thinking, so why do you add Sumi Mountain?"

"Put it all down."

The monk was puzzled, so he said, "Without thinking, how do you put it all down?"

"Then pick it up and carry it away."

1. *Without thinking, is there a mistake or not?*
2. *Un Mun said, "Sumi Mountain." What does this mean?*
3. *"Put it all down." What does this mean?*
4. *"Pick it up and carry it away." What does this mean?*

COMMENTARY: A dog is barking, "Woof, woof"; a rooster is crowing, "Cock-a-doodle-doo"; a cat purrs, "Meow, meow." All animals understand their correct speech.

What is your true speech? Open your mouth, and it's already a mistake; close your mouth, it's also a mistake. What can you do? If you remain silent, then Un Mun's stick has already given you thirty blows. What do you say? If you put it all down, then everything is already yours.

8. Shoot Two Geese

During a stay at the Empty Gate Zen Center in Berkeley, Zen Master Seung Sahn told the following story: "One day, a hunter was walking in a field. Suddenly, two geese flew overhead. He reached for an arrow and shot it from his bow. One goose fell. The hunter wanted to shoot again, but he had no more arrows. So he drew his empty bow and shot. The second goose also fell."

1. *The hunter shot the second goose with an empty bow and the goose fell. How do you shoot the empty bow?*

COMMENTARY: One day, a father and his son go for a drive. Their car is hit by a truck. The father is killed, and the son is taken to the hospital. When the son is wheeled into the emergency room, one of the doctors gasps, shouting, "Oh my God, that's my son!" How could that be?

9. *Past Mind, Present Mind, Future Mind Cannot Get Enlightenment*

The great Sutra Master Dok Sahn was very famous throughout China for his knowledge of the Diamond Sutra. For years he always carried it wherever he went, stopping at temples and lecture halls throughout the country. One day, he learned that there was a temple in the South where the monks did nothing all day but sit facing the wall and sleep, and they still got enlightenment. "That's crazy," Dok Sahn thought. "They don't understand Buddha's teaching, Buddha's actions, or Buddha's mind. How can they get enlightenment? I'll go hit them, wake them up, and teach them the way of the sutras."

So he walked south several hundred miles. One afternoon, he decided to rest for a little while at a small tea house. It was past lunch time, and he was very hungry. The owner, an old woman, was honored to have such a great monk stop at her tea house. She bowed to him and said, "Good afternoon, great monk! Where are you coming from?"

"From the North."

"Where are you going?"

"South."

"Why are you going south?

"I am a Diamond Sutra Master," Dok Sahn replied. "At a temple in the South, the monks only sit facing the wall, sleep, and still get enlightenment. That's crazy! So I will go hit them, wake them up and teach them the Diamond Sutra."

"Oh, that's wonderful!" the woman said. "You are a Diamond Sutra Master! Well, I have a question for you. If you answer correctly, your lunch is free. But if you are wrong, I cannot serve you any lunch."

Dok Sahn grew very angry at this. "Shut up! You are speaking to a Diamond Sutra Master! My knowledge of it is unparalleled throughout the land! Ask me anything!"

"Good," the woman said. "Now, the Diamond Sutra says, 'Past mind cannot get enlightenment, present mind cannot get enlightenment, and future mind cannot get enlightenment.' So I ask you, with what kind of mind will you eat lunch?"

Dok Sahn's jaw dropped. He stammered but could not answer and his face turned red. He was completely stuck. The old woman said, "You've studied the great Diamond Sutra for ten years! If you cannot answer this question, how will you teach the sleeping monks of the South?"

1. *This world is complete stillness. Where do north and south come from?*
2. *What is mind?*
3. *The woman asked, "Past mind cannot get enlightenment, present mind cannot get enlightenment, and future mind cannot get enlightenment. With what kind of mind will you eat lunch?" If you were Dok Sahn, what could you do?*

COMMENTARY: Silence is better than holiness, so one action is better than all the sutras. If you are attached to words and speech, you won't understand a melon's taste; you will only understand its outside form. If you want to understand a melon's taste, then cut a piece and put it in your mouth. A melon grows and ripens by itself; it never explains to human beings its situation and condition.

If you are attached to the sutras, you only understand Buddha's speech. If you want to attain Buddha's mind, then from moment to moment put down your opinion, condition and situation. Only help all beings. Then Buddha appears in front of you. This is enlightenment and freedom from life and death.

10. The Old Woman Burns the Hermitage

It is said that if you practice hard for ten years you will attain something. So, as is customary among many Buddhist laypeople, an old woman in China once supported a monk for ten years. She provided him with food and clothing, and allowed him to live in a hermitage that she provided. For his part, the monk only practiced very, very hard, and did not have to concern himself with anything else.

After ten years, however, there was still no news from the monk. "What did he attain?" she wondered. "I must test this monk." So one afternoon, the woman summoned her sixteen-year-old daughter, who was considered one of the most beautiful girls in the village. Her mother asked her to put on makeup, her best perfume, and clothing made of the finest materials. Then she gave her daughter instructions for testing the monk, loaded her up with plenty of fine food and clothing, and sent her off to the hermitage. The woman's daughter was very excited about the plan!

When she arrived at the hermitage, she bowed to the monk and said, "You have been here for ten years, so my mother made this special food and clothing for you."

"Oh, thank you very much," the monk replied. "Your mother is a great Bodhisattva for supporting me like this for so long."

Just then, the girl strongly embraced the monk, kissed him, and said, "How do you feel now?"

"Rotten log on cold rocks. No warmth in winter."

Releasing him, the girl bowed deeply and said, "You are certainly a great monk!" She returned home, full of happiness and admiration, to report the incident to her mother. "Mother, Mother! This monk's center is very strong, his mind is not moving! He must have attained something!"

"It doesn't matter if his center is very strong, or if his mind cannot be moved, or if he is a wonderful monk. What I want to know is, what did he say?"

"Oh, his words were also wonderful, Mother. He said, 'Rotten log on cold rocks. No warmth in winter.'"

"What!?" the old woman shouted. Fuming, she grabbed a big stick, ran to the hermitage and mercilessly beat the monk, shouting, "Go away! Get out of here! I've spent ten years helping a demon!" Then she burned the hermitage to the ground.

1. *What kind of practice did this monk do for ten years?*
2. *The girl strongly embraced the monk and said, "How do you feel now?" If you were the monk, what could you do?*
3. *Where is the monk's mistake?*

4. *What did the old woman attain that made her beat the monk?*
5. *If you were the old woman and the monk said, "Rotten log on cold rocks. No warmth in winter," what kind of teaching could you give him?*

COMMENTARY: Mother has mother's job, daughter has daughter's job, businessman has businessman's job, monk has monk's job. If you don't understand your job, you don't understand your responsibility.

This monk sat for ten years. What is his job? If you are holding something, and attached to something, then you lose your original job. Put it all down, then your original job and your correct situation, correct relationship, and correct function will appear clearly.

If you understand one, you lose everything. If you attain one, then you get everything. Be careful! What are you doing now? Just do it.

11. *Why Do You Have Five Fingers?*

During a Dharma talk at the Cambridge Zen Center, Zen Master Seung Sahn said to the assembly, "Human beings have one head, two arms, one body and two legs." Then he asked:

1. *Why do you have five fingers?*
2. *Why do you have two legs?*

COMMENTARY: Originally, there are no eyes, no ears, no nose, no tongue, no body and no mind, which means originally no color, no sound, no smell, no taste, no touch and no object of mind. Mind appears, everything appears. Mind disappears, and everything disappears. When mind is clear, everything is clear, and when mind is not clear, everything is not clear.

See clearly, hear clearly, think clearly. Don't be attached to name and form. If your mind is clear like space then everything is reflected: the sky is blue, the tree is green, the dog is barking, "Woof, woof." This is truth. If you attain the function of truth, that is correct life: If someone is hungry, give them food; if someone is thirsty, give them a drink. Just help.

12. How Do You Get Out of the Net?

One day, Zen Master Man Gong sat on the high rostrum and gave the Hae Jae Dharma speech to mark the end of the three-month winter Kyol Che. "All of you sat in the Dharma Room for three months. That is very, very wonderful. As for me, I only stayed in my room making a net. This net is made from a special string. It is very strong and can catch Buddha, Dharma, Bodhisattvas, human beings – everything. How do you get out of this net?"

Some students shouted, "KATZ!" Others hit the floor, or raised a fist, or said, "The sky is blue, the tree is green." One said, "Already got out. How are you, great Zen Master?" while another shouted from the back of the room, "Don't make net!"

Many answers were given, but to each Man Gong only responded, "Aha! I've caught a big fish!"

1. *How do you get out of Zen Master Man Gong's net?*

COMMENTARY: Don't make anything. If you make something, then something is a hindrance. The sky is always bright. Clouds appear and the sky is dark. The wind blows and the clouds disappear. When you put down your opinions and conditions, the correct situation, correct relationship and correct function will appear. If you are attached to speech and words then you are already dead. Be careful.

Understand that to return to primary point, you must begin at 0°, go around the circle, and return to 360°.*

---

*For an explanation of the Zen Circle, see kong-an #37, "The Zen Circle."

13. *No Hindrance*

One day, a nun visited Zen Master Song Sahn. "What is Dharma?" she asked.

"No hindrance."

"Then what does 'no hindrance' mean?"

Song Sahn replied, "Why do you wear clothes?"

At this, the nun stripped naked and walked to the door.

1. *What is Dharma?*
2. *If you were Zen Master Song Sahn, at that time what would you do?*
3. *The nun stripped naked. Is that no hindrance?*

COMMENTARY: A tree understands tree's job, and water understands water's job. What is a Zen Master's job? What is a nun's correct job? If you are attached to speech you will go to hell like an arrow. If you digest speech you can kill all Buddhas and Bodhisattvas. Which one do you like? Put it all down. Go to the store and drink iced tea.

14. *Where Does the Bell Sound Come From?*

One day, as the big temple bell was being rung, the Buddha asked Ananda, "Where does the bell sound come from?"

"The bell."

The Buddha said, "The bell? But if there were no bell stick, how would the sound appear?"

Ananda hastily corrected himself. "The stick! The stick!"

"The stick? If there were no air, how could the sound come here?"

"Yes! Of course! It comes from the air!"

The Buddha asked, "Air? But unless you have an ear, you cannot hear the bell sound."

"Yes! I need an ear to hear it. So it comes from my ear."

The Buddha replied, "Your ear? If you have no consciousness, how can you understand the bell sound?"

"My consciousness makes the sound."

"Your consciousness? So, Ananda, if you have no mind, how do you hear the bell sound?"

"It was created by mind alone."

1. *Everything is created by mind alone. Is that correct?*
2. *If you have no mind, where does the bell sound go?*
3. *Where does the bell sound come from?*

COMMENTARY: True form is without thinking. Truth is unmoving. Name and form, appearing and disappearing - these things never existed. Time and space are always moving. The world of name is the world of opposites. If you are not thinking there are no opposites. See, hear, smell, speak, act, and think clearly.

雨滴聲 | ## 15. Bring This Sound Here

Many students visited Zen Master Kyong Bong at the Absolute Bliss Zen Center in Tong Do Sah Temple. After they bowed to the Zen Master, he asked them, "How are you?"

One student responded, "Fine. And you?"

Kyong Bong said, "Give me your hand."

Then he held the student's hand, palm up, slapped it and said, "Catch this sound and bring it to me."

1. *If you were the student, how could you catch this sound and bring it to the Zen Master?*
2. *The Hua Yen Sutra says, "All things are created by mind alone." Then is this sound created by mind as well?*

COMMENTARY: The spring wind brings flowers, summer wind brings rain, autumn wind brings fruit, and winter wind brings snow. If you want the sound to become yours, then speech and words cannot help you. If you are attached to speech and words, that's already a big mistake.

16. How Many Steps Did You Take to Get Here?

A monk visited Zen Master Kyong Bong and asked, "What is Truth?"
"Where are you coming from?"
"Pusan."

"Oh, that's very far away," Kyong Bong replied. "How many steps did you take to get here?"

1. *If you were the monk, how would you answer?*

COMMENTARY: East wind blowing, cloud goes west; south wind blowing, cloud goes north. Rounding a corner, the bus honks its horn, "Beep, beep." What can you do? You already understand. But be careful of the fish hook. Enough-mind fish never touches the hook. Swimming in the ocean means freedom everywhere.

17. How Do You Clean Your Mind?

Diamond Mountain is a famous mountain in Korea. Near the summit, there was an old Zen center named Maha Yon, and at the bottom was a sutra temple named Yu Jom Sah, where nearly 500 monks studied sutras. Halfway up the mountain, between Maha Yon and Yu Jom Sah, was the famous Diamond Mountain Hot Spring. The owner of the hot spring was a Buddhist laywoman who always let monks in, free of charge.

One day a famous sutra master from Yu Jom Sah, named Sol Hae, came to use the hot spring After he finished bathing, he complimented the owner, "Oh, thank you very much. Excellent springs! Your hot tub is the best in the world."

"You're welcome," the owner replied. "Your face looks very wonderful! Now, I have a question for you: You cleaned your body in the hot tub. How do you clean your mind?"

Sol Hae was stuck.

1. *What is mind?*
2. *Body and mind – are they the same or different?*
3. *If you were the great sutra master, how would you answer?*

COMMENTARY: The Sixth Patriarch said that originally there is nothing. So if you make something, you hinder something. If you want to understand the realm of the Buddhas then keep a mind which is clear like space. Then your mind is like a clear mirror: red comes, red is reflected; white comes, white. Anything coming and going is no hindrance. If you have mind, you must clean it. If you have no mind, cleaning is not necessary. Put it down – that will help your life.

18. Great Teacher Bu Dae Sa Expounds the Diamond Sutra

Emperor Yang Mu Je requested Great Teacher Bu Dae Sa to expound the Diamond Sutra. The Great Teacher climbed onto the high rostrum, shook the desk once, and then got down off the seat. Emperor Yang Mu Je was astonished. Master Ji Gang asked him, "Does your majesty understand?"

The Emperor said, "No, I do not understand."

"The Great Teacher Bu Dae Sa has finished expounding the sutra," Master Ji Gang said.

1. *Why did the Great Teacher Bu Dae Sa shake his desk once?*
2. *Emperor Yang Mu Je said, "I don't understand." What does this mean?*
3. *Master Ji Gang said, "The Great Teacher Bu Dae Sa has finished expounding the sutra." What does this mean?*

COMMENTARY: Do you see? Do you hear? The sun, the moon, the stars, the trees and the rivers are already teaching us the Diamond Sutra. If you open your mouth, you lose the Diamond Sutra's true meaning. Just seeing, just hearing, just smelling is better than the Diamond Sutra. The rooster crows,

"Cock-a-doodle-doo." The dog barks, "Woof, woof." Is that the Diamond Sutra or not? Don't check, put it down. What are you doing now? Just do it.

19. How Do You Clean Dust?

A renowned Dharma Master from Hong Kong named Sae Jin once gave a Dharma talk at the New York Zen Center. After the talk, he asked for questions. People raised many interesting questions about his talk, to which he gave insightful answers. Finally, one student asked him, "Your name is 'Sae Jin,' which means 'Clean Dust,' but the Sixth Patriarch said, 'Originally nothing. Where is dust?' So, how can you clean dust?"

Sae Jin was stuck. Although his understanding was great, he only understood the sutras, but did not understand Zen, so he couldn't say anything.

1. *The Sixth Patriarch said, "Originally nothing." What does this mean?*
2. *The student asked, "Your name is 'Sae Jin,' which means 'Clean Dust.' . . . How can you clean dust?" If you were Sae Jin, what could you do?*

COMMENTARY: The Sixth Patriarch wrote a poem:

> Bodhi has no tree.
> Clear mirror has no stand.
> Originally nothing.
> Where is dust?

So originally there is nothing. Where does Bodhi come from? Where does the clear mirror come from? If you are originally nothing, how can you even say, "Originally nothing? Where is dust?" That is a big mistake. If you attain the Sixth Patriarch's mistake then you attain his true meaning, and these questions are no hindrance. But you must hit the Sixth Patriarch's mistake. That is very necessary.

20. Not Attached to Anything, Thinking Arises

A long time ago in China, before he became the Sixth Patriarch, Layman No worked in the mountains every day, gathering firewood to sell in the city. He would use the money he made to buy food, clothing and whatever else was needed to help his mother. He worked only to support her.

One afternoon, on his way back from town, he came upon a monk who was reciting the Diamond Sutra. Layman No stood still and quietly listened, hearing the line, "Not attached to anything, thinking arises." At this, he suddenly got the Great Enlightenment.

1. *"Not attached to anything, thinking arises." What does this mean?*
2. *What did he attain?*
3. *What is the Great Enlightenment?*

COMMENTARY: If you have no "I-me-my," then moment-to-moment, keeping correct situation, correct relationship, and correct function is possible. If you are holding something or attached to something, when you die you will go straight to hell. Layman No worked every day only for his mother. He heard one word and understood himself. If you don't hold anything, you can also attain your true self and freedom from life and death. That is very, very wonderful!

21. See True Buddha

The Diamond Sutra says, "All formations are impermanent. If you view all appearance as non-appearance, then you can see true Buddha."

But everything is impermanent, so Buddha is impermanent, and you are also impermanent. How can impermanence see impermanence? Therefore, the sentence in the Diamond Sutra should be changed to "If you view all appearance as non-appearance, this view is Buddha."

1. *How do you view all appearance as non-appearance?*
2. *What is "true Buddha"?*
3. *"This view is Buddha." What does this mean?*

COMMENTARY: Before you are born, there are no six roots, six consciousnesses, or six dusts. After you are born, these six roots, consciousnesses, and dusts control you. This is suffering. If you control them, then nothing is a hindrance: you are already beyond life and death. Moment to moment, only help all beings. This is the great Bodhisattva Way.

22. *This Stillness Is Bliss*

The Mahaparinirvana Sutra says, "All things are appearing and disappearing. That is the law of appearing and disappearing. When both appearing and disappearing disappear, this stillness is bliss."

All human beings have two bodies: a form-body and a Dharma-body. The form-body is always appearing and disappearing, so it is always suffering and therefore it cannot attain true bliss. The Dharma-body never appears or disappears, so it has no form, feelings, perceptions, impulses or consciousness. It is like the rocks and the trees; therefore it, too, cannot get bliss.

1. *What is the law of appearing and disappearing?*
2. *How do "both appearing and disappearing disappear"?*
3. *Are the form-body and the Dharma-body the same or different?*
4. *What kind of body gets "stillness is bliss"?*

COMMENTARY: A long time ago in China, there was a Sutra Master named Ji Do who studied the Mahaparinirvana Sutra for ten years. He understood that the form-body cannot get bliss because it is always appearing and disappearing, but he still could not understand how the Dharma-body gets bliss, since it has no feelings and is like the rocks and trees. So Ji Do had a big question: "How does the Dharma-body get bliss?"

In order to find an explanation, he visited the Sixth Patriarch. The Sixth Patriarch asked him, "Is it your form-body or Dharma-body which is asking this question? If it is your form-body, then you appear and disappear; if it your Dharma-body, you are like the rocks and the trees, and you cannot hear my speech. What do you say?" Ji Do was completely stuck. Then the Sixth Patriarch said, "Don't make anything!" Ji Do heard this and was instantly enlightened.

23. *Is Your Body Form or Emptiness?*

The Heart Sutra says, "Avalokiteshvara Bodhisattva perceives that all five *skandhas* are empty." So form is emptiness, emptiness is form. Originally, there are no eyes, no ears, no nose, no tongue, no body, and no mind.

1. *Is your body form or emptiness?*
2. *"All five skandhas are empty." What does this mean?*

COMMENTARY: One mind appears and the whole universe appears. One mind disappears and the whole universe disappears. The clouds float from the ocean, rain falls from the sky.

But if one mind never appears or disappears, then what? What do you see now? What do you hear now? Your mind is like a clear mirror. The mountain is blue, water is flowing.

24. *What Is Insight?*

There are three kinds of practice in Theravada Buddhism:

Sila – Precepts
Samadhi – Meditation
Prajna – Wisdom

If you practice these three things, you get insight into impermanence, insight into impurity and insight into non-self.

1. *What is insight into impermanence?*
2. *What is insight into impurity?*
3. *What is insight into non-self?*
4. *There are three kinds of insight. Are they the same or different?*
5. *When you see the mountain and the river, what kind of insight is this?*

COMMENTARY: The dog is barking, "Woof, woof"; the rooster is crowing, "Cock-a-doodle-doo!" Are these coming or going? Are they inside or outside your mind, pure or impure? Don't make anything! If you make something, you lose your life. Without making anything, you are already complete.

25. *Nirvana and Annutara Samyak Sambodhi*

The Heart Sutra says that there is no cognition, and no attainment with nothing to attain. Next, it says, "the Bodhisattva depends on Prajna Paramita and . . . dwells in Nirvana." Finally, it says, "In the three worlds all Buddhas depend on Prajna Paramita and attain Annutara Samyak Sambodhi."

1. *What is Nirvana?*
2. *What is Annutara Samyak Sambodhi?*
3. *If there is "No cognition and no attainment, with nothing to attain," how do all Buddhas attain Annutara Samyak Sambodhi?*

4. *"The Bodhisattva depends on Prajna Paramita and . . . dwells in Nirvana." "All Buddhas depend on Prajna Paramita and attain Annutara Samyak Sambodhi." If you depend on Prajna Paramita, what do you get?*

5. *What do you depend on?*

COMMENTARY: "Form is emptiness. Emptiness is form." This is the world of opposites. "No form. No emptiness." This is Nirvana, the absolute world. "Form is form. Emptiness is emptiness." This is Annutara Samyak Sambodhi, or the complete world.

Are these three the same or different? If you don't understand, then you must find some meat and give it to a hungry dog. This dog will teach you the true meaning of the Heart Sutra.

26. All Things Are Created by Mind Alone

The Hua Yen (Avatamsaka) Sutra says, "If you wish to thoroughly understand all Buddhas of the past, present and future, then you should view the nature of the whole universe as being created by mind alone."

1. *Are there differences between past, present and future Buddhas?*

2. *What is "the nature of the whole universe"?*

3. *Mind created everything. What created mind?*

COMMENTARY: A long time ago in Korea, a famous Sutra Master named Dae Oh Sunim traveled to Hae In Sah Temple to lecture on the Hua Yen Sutra. He concluded his week's teaching by stating, "For forty-nine years, the Buddha taught only one word: 'All things are created by mind alone.'"

After the talk, there were many questions and answers. Then one young Zen monk stood up and asked, "You said that all things are created by mind alone. My question is: where does this mind come from?" Dae Oh Sunim was completely stuck, and could not answer.

Do you understand? If not, go ask a tree. The tree will answer for you.

27. *The Stone Man Is Crying*

As a young monk, Zen Master Man Gong was asked, "The ten thousand dharmas return to the One. Where does the One return?" He could not answer this question, and for a long time it would not let him go. Then one day, he heard the sound of the temple bell, and got enlightenment. Overjoyed, and very confident, he went around from temple to temple and met with many Sutra Masters. He asked one of them, "The Lotus Sutra talks about the Dharma. Where does this Dharma come from?" The Sutra Master could not answer. Man Gong hit him and said, "That is Dharma. You should understand that."

He asked another temple's Sutra Master, "The Hua Yen Sutra talks about mind. What is mind?" The Sutra Master could not answer him, so Man Gong hit him, too.

He went all around hitting many Sutra Masters. Man Gong had too much pride, thinking, "I already got enlightenment." Eventually he met Zen Master Kyong Ho at Ma Gok Sah Temple. "Man Gong Sunim, I heard you got enlightenment," the famous Master said.

"Yes, I did."

"Then I have something to ask you. This is a brush. This is paper. Are they the same or different?"

Man Gong thought, "That's no problem, very easy," and replied, "The paper is the brush, the brush is the paper."

"Then I ask you: The paper and the brush come from where?"

Man Gong shouted, "KATZ!"

"Not good, not bad," Kyong Ho said, and asked several more questions, which Man Gong answered easily. Finally, Kyong Ho asked, "The traditional funeral ceremony chant says, 'The stone man is crying.' What does this mean?"

Man Gong was stuck. He had never heard this kind of question before. His mind became tight, and all his pride vanished. Kyong Ho shouted at him, "You don't understand this meaning! How can you say, 'The brush is the paper, the paper is the brush'?"

Man Gong bowed deeply and said, "I'm sorry. Please teach me."

"A long time ago, a monk asked Zen Master Joju, 'Does a dog have Buddha nature?' Joju said, 'Mu.' Do you understand that?"

"I don't know."

Then Kyong Ho said, "Only go straight, don't know! OK?"

For the next three years, Man Gong did very hard training, always keeping only don't-know. One day, he was sitting at Tong Do Sah's Absolute Bliss Zen Center. Again, he heard the sound of a bell and this time got complete enlightenment. He sent a letter to Kyong Ho that said, "Thank you very much for your great teaching. Now I understand: kimchee is hot, sugar is sweet."

Zen Master Kyong Ho was very happy, and gave Dharma Transmission to Man Gong.

1. *Brush and paper: are they the same or different?*
2. *Man Gong shouted, "KATZ!" What does this mean?*
3. *"The stone man is crying." What does this mean?*
4. *Man Gong first heard the bell and got enlightenment. Later, he heard the bell and again got enlightenment. His first enlightenment and his second enlightenment — how are they different?*
5. *"Kimchee is hot. Sugar is sweet." What does this mean?*

COMMENTARY: $1 + 2 = 3$. $3 \times 0 = 0$. $3 \times 3 = 9$. Are these the same or different? If you say the same, you don't understand mathematics. If you say different, you also don't understand mathematics. $10,000 \times 0 = 0$. Mountain $\times 0 = 0$. Water $\times 0 = 0$. Is that correct? But what is mountain x mountain? What is water x water? It's very clear – the correct answer already appears.

Where is Man Gong's first mistake? When did Man Gong completely attain? You already understand. When standing in front of the Buddha if you hear the sound of the moktak, just bow. That is your original face.

28. Three Statements

The *Compass of Zen* says that there are three kinds of Zen:

Theoretical Zen teaches, "Form is emptiness. Emptiness is form."

Tathagata Zen teaches, "No form. No emptiness."

Patriarchal Zen teaches, "Form is form. Emptiness is emptiness."

1. Which one is correct?
2. "Form is emptiness. Emptiness is form." What does this mean?
3. "No form. No emptiness." What does this mean?
4. "Form is form. Emptiness is emptiness." What does this mean?

COMMENTARY: Mountain is water, water is mountain. But originally there is nothing. If you don't make anything, then no mountain and no water. Then your mind is clear like space, which means it is clear like a mirror: mountain is mountain, water is water. The mirror correctly reflects everything.

Of these three statements, which one is correct? If you find the correct one, you lose your life; if you cannot find it, you lose your body. What can you do? Go drink tea – then it's clearly in front of you: mountain is blue, water is flowing.

29. Not Depending on Anything

Not depending on words, a special transmission outside the sutras, pointing directly to mind: see your true nature, become Buddha.

1. What is "a special transmission outside the sutras"?
2. How do you point directly to mind?

3. *"See your true nature, become Buddha."* What does this mean?

COMMENTARY: This world was originally complete stillness. That means there were no names, no forms, no words. If mind appears, then the sky, the earth, the mountains, the rivers, everything appears. If mind disappears, where do these things return to? If you say, "They return to emptiness," then you have opened your mouth, which is already a mistake. What can you do? If you don't understand, go to the kitchen and drink cold water.

30. What Do You Need?

The Buddha taught all the Dharmas in order to save all minds. When you do not keep all these minds, what use is there for the Dharmas?

1. *How do you not keep all these minds?*
2. *What use is there for the Dharmas?*
3. *Is mind first or Dharma first?*
4. *No Dharma, no mind. Then what?*

COMMENTARY: Mind appears, Dharma appears. Dharma appears – like, dislike, coming, going, life and death – all these things appear. When mind disappears, then everything disappears, speech and words also disappear. Opening your mouth is a big mistake. What can you do? Put it all down. Don't touch the fish hook. When you are hungry, just eat. When you are thirsty, just drink.

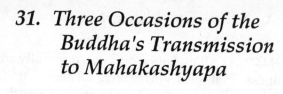

31. Three Occasions of the Buddha's Transmission to Mahakashyapa

I. One morning, the Buddha sat in front of the Pagoda of Many Children. Many disciples had gathered from near and far to hear his Dharma speech. Everyone waited for him to begin, but the Buddha did not open his mouth. In the front rows were the older students, including many venerable monks. The new monks and novices sat far away in the back. Mahakashyapa arrived and walked to the front, in front of the Buddha. Though he was an old man, he had only recently become a monk, so everyone thought it was incorrect of him to walk in front of the Buddha. But when the Buddha saw him, he moved over and allowed Mahakashyapa to sit next to him on his cushion. Everyone was surprised and amazed. By this action, the Buddha was demonstrating the equality of dharma nature.

II. The Buddha was at Vulture's Peak. Over a thousand disciples were assembled to hear him speak, but he did not open his mouth. After several minutes of silence, he held up a flower before the assembly. No one understood. Only Mahakashyapa smiled. Then the Buddha said, "I transmit my true Dharma to you."

III. The Buddha died when he was eighty years old. In those days, people often lived to one hundred, so many of his disciples did a lot of checking: "Why did the Buddha die?" "Why didn't he live longer?" "This is not fair." Furthermore, they could not begin the funeral ceremony without the Buddha's great disciple, Mahakashyapa. They anxiously waited seven days, when finally Mahakashyapa arrived. The wood was stacked high for the funeral pyre and on top was the gold coffin containing the Buddha's body. Perceiving that everyone was still sad and confused, Mahakashyapa bowed three times in front of the pyre, walked clockwise around it three times, and bowed in front of it three times.

After the last bow, there was a big clap of thunder. The coffin broke open and the Buddha's feet appeared. Everyone was very shocked and instantly realized this teaching:

Only the Buddha's body had died, but the true Buddha never dies.

I. a. *Mahakashyapa sat next to the Buddha. What does this mean?*

b. *What is the equality of dharma nature?*

II. a. *Why did Mahakashyapa smile?*

b. *What kind of Dharma was transmitted to him?*

III. a. *The Buddha's feet broke through the coffin. What does this mean?*

b. *"Only the Buddha's body had died, but the true Buddha never dies." What does this mean?*

COMMENTARY: The Buddha and Mahakashyapa are good actors. But nobody understands their meaning: Only the Buddha and Mahakashyapa understand each other, so they are *not* good actors. If you have neither the Buddha nor Mahakashyapa, then everything is very clear: the sky is blue, the tree is green, water is flowing. You can see clearly, you can hear clearly.

But the Buddha and Mahakashyapa take away all of their students' eyes, ears, noses, and mouths. This is a number one bad job. If you attain this "bad job" then you are better than the Buddha and Mahakashyapa. How wonderful!

32. *Pointing Directly to Mind*

A long time ago in China, Zen Master Dong Sahn was asked, "What is Buddha?" He answered, "Three pounds of flax." When someone asked Zen Master Un Mun the same question, he replied, "Dry shit on a stick," and when Zen Master Joju was asked, "Why did Bodhidharma come to China?" he answered, "The cypress tree in the garden."

1. *"What is Buddha?"* Zen Master Dong Sahn answered, *"Three pounds of flax."* That is only 80 percent correct. What is 100 percent?
2. *"What is Buddha?"* Zen Master Un Mun answered, *"Dry shit on a stick."* That was a big mistake. Where is the mistake?
3. When Zen Master Joju was asked, *"Why did Bodhidharma come to China?"* he answered, *"The cypress tree in the garden."* That was not correct. How can you make it correct?

COMMENTARY: If you are attached to speech, then you lose your life. If you perceive speech then you understand correct situation. If you understand the correct function of speech, then you will get complete freedom from life and death. Ice becomes water, water becomes steam. So, ice, water and steam – are they the same or different? If you say "the same" you lose your mouth. If you say "different" your mouth goes to hell. What can you do? Hear clearly, smell clearly, think clearly – then you will attain the truth and the correct way. Be careful of your ears. If you are attached to speech, you will go to hell like an arrow.

33. See True Nature, Become Buddha

1. *The willow is green, the flowers are red. Is that nature or is that Buddha?*
2. *The crow is black, the crane is white. Do you see Buddha? Do you hear nature?*

COMMENTARY: The Diamond Sutra says that all formations are always appearing and disappearing. If you view all appearances as non-appearances, then you can see Buddha. If you want to see Buddha, Buddha has already disappeared. If you don't want to see Buddha, then seeing, hearing, smelling, touching, tasting – everything is Buddha. The flower is red, the tree is green, the sky is blue. You and these things are never separate. Then you are Buddha.

34. Great Enlightenment

Heaven earth, earth heaven, heaven earth
revolve.
Water mountain, mountain water, water
mountain emptiness.
Heaven heaven, earth earth, when did they ever
revolve?
Mountain mountain, water water, each is
separate from the other.

There are three kinds of enlightenment. First Enlightenment means "Primary Point." Original Enlightenment is "Like-This," which means truth. Final Enlightenment is "Just-Like-This," which means correct function is correct life.

1. *What is "Primary Point"?*
2. *What does "Like-This" mean?*
3. *What does "Just-Like-This" mean?*
4. *Of the four lines in the poem above, which one is Great Enlightenment?*

COMMENTARY: In the spring, the fog is so dense you cannot see through it. In the summer, there is much rain. In the fall, many clouds come and go quickly. In the winter, snow falls everywhere. Fog, rain, clouds, and snow – are they the same or different? Where do they come from? If you say they are the same, you have already lost your tongue. If you say they are different, you lose your body. What can you do? $1 + 2 = 3$, $3 \times 3 = 9$, but $9 \times 0 = 0$. If you attain that number then your true face is in front of you. How wonderful!

35. The Three Essential Elements of Zen

There are three essential elements of Zen:
Great Faith
Great Courage
Great Question

If you have Great Faith, you attain correct way.
If you have Great Courage, you attain truth.
If you have Great Question, you attain correct life.

Having Great Faith is like a hen sitting on her eggs to keep them warm. She always keeps her direction, never moving, no matter what.

Having Great Courage is like a cat catching a mouse. The cat focuses one hundred percent of its strength and attention on one point and one action: first on waiting, then on pouncing.

Having Great Question is like a person who has not eaten in three days, who only thinks of food. Or it is like someone who is thirsty, having worked all day in the hot sun with nothing to drink, and who thinks only of water. Or it is like a child whose mother is far away: this child wants his mother, and his mind thinks only of her. Great Question is single-mindedness, a mind that is focused on only one thing.

1   *What is Great Faith?*
2.   *What is Great Courage?*
3.   *What is Great Question?*

COMMENTARY: One, two, three. Where do these numbers come from? You already understand. Children want candy; businesspeople want money; scholars want to become famous. There are many kinds of people and many directions. Where do they finally go? If you attain this point, you attain human nature and universal substance. If you attain universal substance, you can see and hear clearly, and your emotions, will, and wisdom can function correctly. Then your life is correct and you can help all beings. This is called the Great Bodhisattva Way.

36. *Energy in Zen*

When walking, standing, sitting, lying down, speaking, being silent, moving, being still, at all times, in all places, without interruption, what is this?

One mind is infinite kalpas.

1. *"All times" and "all places" come from where?*
2. *"One mind is infinite kalpas." Are infinite kalpas inside or outside this one mind?*
3. *What is one mind?*
4. *What are "infinite kalpas"?*

COMMENTARY: The Avatamsaka Sutra says, "If you wish to thoroughly understand all the Buddhas of the past, present and future, then you should view the nature of the whole universe as being created by mind alone." If you have no mind, where can the Buddha stay? Who comes? Who goes? If "one mind" disappears, where are time and space? Put it down, then everything is clear. The mountain is blue, water is flowing.

37. The Zen Circle

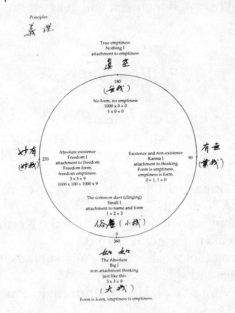

We sometimes explain Zen by means of a circle. The circle has five points: 0°, 90°, 180°, 270° and 360°.

0° is "Small I."
90° is "Karma I."
180° is "Nothing I."
270° is "Freedom I."
360° is "Big I."

1. *What is the meaning of "Small I"?*
2. *What is the meaning of "Karma I"?*
3. *What is the meaning of "Nothing I"?*
4. *What is the meaning of "Big I"?*
5. *"Big I" and "Small I" are at the same point. Are "Big I" and "Small I" the same or different?*
7. *If "Small I" disappears, what?*
8. *"Small I," "Karma I," "Nothing I," "Freedom I" and "Big I." Which one is the true "I"?*

COMMENTARY: If one mind appears then everything appears. If one mind disappears then everything disappears. All these degrees and these "I"s come from where? You already understand. But no mind, no eyes – then what? What do you see now? Is that "Big I" or "Small I"? Put it all down! Just see, just hear and then you will get everything.

| 38. *Five Schools*

The Sixth Patriarch Hui Neng's two more prominent disciples, Ch'ing Yuan and Nan Yeh, gave birth to five major schools of Zen:

1. Im Je (Rinzai) School: Whole substance, correct function is KATZ or Hit.
2. Un Mun School: Body hidden in the North Star but appears in the golden wind.
3. Jo Dong (Soto) School: King and subjects together, center and sides never separate.
4. Poep Ahn School: Hear sound, attain correct way, mind is clear.
5. Wi Ahn School: Teacher and student in harmony together. Father and son live in the same house.

1. *What is the meaning of the Im Je School?*
2. *What is the meaning of the Un Mun School?*
3. *What is the meaning of the Jo Dong School?*
4. *What is the meaning of the Poep Ahn School?*
5. *What is the meaning of the Wi Ahn School?*

COMMENTARY: One body, five heads. Where does it go? Go straight: Only depend on your legs.

39. What Is Buddha-Nature?

The Buddha said that all things have Buddha-nature. Zen Master Joju said that a dog has no Buddha-nature.

1. *Which one is correct?*
2. *Which one is incorrect?*
3. *The ten thousand dharmas return to the One. Where does the One return?*

COMMENTARY: The dog never says, "I am a dog." But the dog is barking. The cat never says, "I am a cat." But the cat is meowing. Name and form do not matter. The dog, the tree and the flower all understand their job, but Buddha doesn't understand Buddha's job; human beings don't understand human being's job. Very stupid! Put it all down. What are you doing now? Just do it! That's all.

40. The Human Route

Coming empty-handed, going empty-handed, that is human.
When you are born, where do you come from?
When you die, where do you go?
Life is like a floating cloud which appears.
Death is like a floating cloud which disappears.
The floating cloud itself originally does not exist.

Life and death, coming and going are also like that. But there is one thing which always remains clear. It is pure and clear, not depending on life and death. Then what is the one pure and clear thing?

1. *When you are born, where do you come from?*
2. *When you die, where do you go?*
3. *What is the one pure and clear thing?*

COMMENTARY: A dog understands a dog's job, and a cat understands a cat's job. Human beings appear – what are they to do? They want fame, money, food, sex, and sleep. After that, then what? But one thing is clear. It swallows everything – the sun, the moon, the stars, the mountains, water – everything. If you find that, you attain "you," and freedom from life and death. Then go drink tea.

41. *Just Seeing Is Buddha-Nature*

If you want to understand the realm of Buddha, keep a mind which is clear like space. Let all thinking and external desires fall far away. Let your mind go any place, with no hindrance. Then what is keeping a mind which is clear like space? If your mind is not clear, listen to the following:

It is enlightenment-nature.
Above is the dwelling place of all Buddhas;
Below are the six realms of existence.
One by one, each thing is complete.
One by one, each thing has it.
It and dust interpenetrate.
It is already apparent in all things.
So, without cultivation, you are already complete –
Understand, understand.
Clear, clear.

(*Holding the Zen stick*) Do you see?

(*Hitting with the Zen stick*) Do you hear?
Already you see clearly. Already you hear clearly.
Then what are this stick, this sound and your mind?
Are they the same or different?
If you say "same," I will hit you thirty times.
If you say "different," I will also hit you thirty times.
Why?
KATZ!
3 x 3 = 9.

1. *How do you keep a mind which is clear like space?*
2. *"Understand, understand, Clear, clear." What does this mean?*
3. *What does "3 x 3 = 9" mean?*

COMMENTARY: In the springtime, many flowers. In the summer, the trees are green. In the fall, fruit appears. In the winter, it is very cold. In the beginning, four legs; next, two legs; next, three legs; next, no legs. Where do they stay? Do you understand that? If you don't understand ask the stone girl. She will have a good answer for you.

| 42. *Where Are You Going?*

Ancient Buddhas went like this.
Present Buddhas go like this.
You go like this.
I also go like this.
What is the thing that is not broken?
Who is eternally indestructible?
Do you understand?
In the three worlds,
all Buddhas of the past, present and future
simultaneously become the Path.
On the ten levels,
all beings on the same day enter Nirvana.

If you don't understand this, check the following:

The statue has eyes and tears silently drip down.
The boy sniffles wordlessly in the dark.

1. *Who is eternally indestructible?*
2. *What do the following sentences mean?*
   a. *In the three worlds,*
      all Buddhas of past, present and future simultaneously
      become the Path.
   b. *The statue has eyes and tears silently drip down.*
   c. *The boy sniffles wordlessly in the dark.*

COMMENTARY: Where does mind come from? Where does
it go? Originally there is no name and no form. Open your
mouth, everything appears. Close your mouth, everything
disappears. If you have no mouth, then what? If you don't
understand, go ask the gold Buddha-statue. He will teach you.

43. *Zen Master To Sol's Three Gates*

Zen Master To Sol had three gates:

1. *Cutting ignorance grass and sitting Zen is wishing to see*
   nature. Then where is your nature now?
2. *You already understand nature and pass beyond life and*
   death. When you die, how will you be reborn?
3. *You already have freedom over life and death and also*
   understand where you return to. When the four elements
   disperse, where do you go?

COMMENTARY: Coming empty-handed, going empty-
handed – that is human. What are empty hands? Where do
these empty hands come from? Who made this? When
thinking appears, everything appears. If you have no thinking,
where will you stay? Put it all down. What are you doing
now? If you are thirsty, go drink cold water.

44. Freedom from Life and Death

Under the sea, a running cow eats the moon.
In front of the rock, the stone tiger sleeps,
    holding a baby in his arms.
The steel snake drills into the eye of a diamond.
Mount Kun-Lun rides on the back of an
    elephant pulled by a little bird.

1. *Which of these sentences is freedom from life and death?*

COMMENTARY: If you want something then you lose everything. If you don't want anything then you already have everything. But you must hear the stone lion roaring. Then the whole world is in your hand. You can be free and can do anything.

45. Quiet Night, the Geese Cry

Sitting silently in a mountain temple in the
    quiet night,
Extreme quiet and stillness are original
    naturalness.
Why does the Western wind shake the forest?
A single cry of the cold-weather geese fills the
    sky.

1. *"Extreme quiet and stillness are original naturalness." What does this mean?*
2. *"Why does the Western wind shake the forest?" What does this mean?*
3. *"A single cry of the cold-weather geese fills the sky." What does this mean?*

COMMENTARY: Bodhidharma came from the West. The Eastern world had many problems, so he sat in Sorim for nine years. That was a big mistake. But this mistake fixed all human beings' mistake. For cold sickness, use cold medicine; hot sickness, use hot medicine. So Bodhidharma's mistake fixed all human beings' mistake. What kind of mistake did Bodhidharma make? Three years after he died, he was alive again, and returned to the West. Where is Bodhidharma now? In front of you the pine tree is green.

46. Zen Master Ko Bong's Three Gates

1. *The sun in the sky shines everywhere. Why does a cloud obscure it?*
2. *Everyone has a shadow following them. How can you not step on your shadow?*
3. *The whole universe is on fire. Through what kind of samadhi can you escape being burned?*

COMMENTARY: The sun, the moon, the stars, the mountains and waters – everything is complete. One mind appears, big mistake. One mind disappears, then seeing and hearing become the truth. Don't make anything. Just see, just hear, just *do* it.

47. Just Like This Is Buddha

The *Compass of Zen* says:

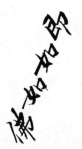

The spirit remains clear and light.
The six roots (senses) and the six dusts
(perceptions) are taken off and thrown
away.
The original body remains clear constantly.
Speech and words cannot hinder it.
True nature has no tint and is already a perfect
sphere.
Only without thinking, just like this is Buddha.

1. *"The original body remains clear constantly."* What does this mean?
2. *"True nature has no tint."* What does this mean?
3. *"Only without thinking, just like this is Buddha."* What does this mean?

COMMENTARY: Everything is already complete, but human beings have one mouth and two eyes. That is a mistake. If you have no sixth consciousness, then are the tree and the rocks the same or different? Seeing and hearing are already a big mistake. Don't check, just do it. Then you are better than Buddha.

48. Where Are the Buddha and the Eminent Teachers?

The four elements (earth, water, fire and air) disperse as in a dream.
The six dusts (perceptions), roots (senses), and consciousnesses are originally empty.
To understand that, the Buddha and the Eminent Teachers return to the place of light:
The sun is setting over the western mountains. The moon is rising in the east.

1. *The six dusts, roots and consciousnesses all disappear. Then what?*
2. *Where are the Buddha and the Eminent Teachers?*
3. *Before the sun sets, before the moon rises — what?*

COMMENTARY: One man has no use for the Buddha. He sees clearly and hears clearly. He never checks, never holds, and is not attached to anything. You, too, just eat, just work, just sleep, just do it. Then all Buddhas become your attendants. How wonderful!

49. Why Are You Saying These Bad Things About Me?

Ko Bong Sunim had been drinking too much liquor. He went to his room and lay down and began saying bad things about his teacher, Zen Master Man Gong. "Man Gong doesn't understand anything. . . . He's not correct. . . . His speech is bullshit."

Just then, Man Gong walked past Ko Bong's room and heard him. He opened the door and shouted, "Ko Bong, why are you saying these bad things about me?"

Surprised, Ko Bong sat up and said, "Zen Master, I am not saying any bad things about *you*. I am only saying these things about Man Gong."

The Zen Master asked, "Man Gong and me, are they the same or different?"

Ko Bong shouted, "KATZ!"

Man Gong smiled. "You've had too much to drink. Now go to sleep."

1. *"Man Gong and me, are they the same or different?" What does this mean?*
2. *Ko Bong shouted, "KATZ!" How many pounds does it weigh?*

COMMENTARY: Ko Bong thinks about this world as if it were a small coin. He sees the road as if it were a thread. All Buddhas and Bodhisattvas are his attendants. His teacher, Man Gong, is like a baby. So, Ko Bong is a great, free person. But he doesn't understand one thing: his condition. He only understands his situation. So who can take care of him? A stone girl appears. She shouts at him, "You must sleep!" Ko Bong only says, "Yes, Ma'am," and goes to sleep.

50. *Ko Bong's Enlightenment*

One summer, before he became a great Zen Master, Ko Bong Sunim sat summer Kyol Che at Tong Do Sah Temple. It was very hot that summer, so many retreatants could not stay in the meditation hall. Some sat on the veranda, some sat under the trees, while others sat by a nearby stream. Ko Bong sat on some rocks, under a big tree, courageously keeping don't-know mind one hundred percent. Above him, a cicada was singing in the tree. Ko Bong heard that and instantly his mind opened – he got enlightenment. He hit the rocks with a fan and the fan broke. "That's it!" he shouted, laughing, "Ha, ha, ha, ha, ha, ha!!"

1. *Ko Bong heard the cicada's song and got enlightenment. What did he attain?*
2. *He hit the rocks with a fan and broke the fan, then shouted, "That's it!" What does this mean?*
3. *Loud laughter: "Ha, ha, ha, ha, ha, ha!!" What does this mean?*

COMMENTARY: One day, sometime before this summer Kyol Che, Ko Bong visited Tong Do Sah Temple. He stood at the gate and shouted, "Somebody come here and cut my hair, please. I want to become a monk." Many monks were angered by his arrogant behavior. They grabbed some sticks and went out to beat him. Ko Bong only said, "You can hit my body but you cannot hit my mind. If you can hit my mind, I will become your disciple." But none of the monks could hit his mind.

Another time, outside Nam Ja Sah Temple, he shouted the same kinds of things, and again all of the monks were very angry and wanted to beat him. Ko Bong again asked if anyone could hit his mind. At that time, Zen Master Hae Bong heard this and came to see Ko Bong. He asked, "How many pounds does your mind weigh?" Ko Bong could not answer, so he cut off all his hair and became a monk.

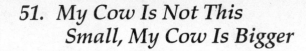

51. My Cow Is Not This Small, My Cow Is Bigger

One summer, Ko Bong Sunim sat Kyol Che at Won Sah Temple, where the famous Zen Master Hae Wol was teaching. There were thirty monks sitting mornings and evenings, and working in the garden during the day. The work was hard and they were all very tired by evening. Also, they had no money and very little food, and the food that they had was awful. There were many complaints among the monks.

One morning, Zen Master Hae Wol left his students for a few days to visit the head temple. After he left, Ko Bong talked his fellow monks into selling the temple's cow. (They needed this cow for work in the garden, so without it, they would not be able to work.) After selling the cow, Ko Bong suggested they buy good food and drink for everyone. That night, instead of sitting, they had a big party. They ate, drank, shouted, danced, and sang songs. They were very happy. They went to sleep quite late and did not get up for morning chanting.

As he returned to the temple early the next morning, with the sun already rising, the Zen Master could not hear any chanting. He noticed that the cow was missing. Upon opening the temple door, he was hit with the bad smell from all the food and drink. His students lay all about, snoring loudly.

Perceiving what they had done, he became very angry and shouted, "Wake up! Wake up!!" Everyone jumped up, very afraid, but could say nothing. Walking toward the Buddha statue, he looked from student to student. His eyes were big, like a lion's. "Who stole my cow?" he shouted. Everyone jumped nervously, and became even more afraid. But they said nothing. They all just looked at Ko Bong Sunim. For his part, Ko Bong just sat there. He was not afraid. Again the Zen Master shouted, "Who stole my cow?"

Ko Bong stood up and removed all his clothes. Getting down on his hands and kneeds he crawled in front of Hae Wol, saying, "Moo! Moooo!"

Zen Master Hae Wol only smiled, and hit Ko Bong on his bare ass, saying, "My cow is not this small." Hitting him again, he added, "My cow is bigger."

Then Ko Bong got up and returned to his room. The cow was never mentioned again.

1. *Ko Bong said, "Moo!" What did he mean?*
2. *Ko Bong's body and the cow's body — are they the same or different?*
3. *Why did the Zen Master never mention the cow again?*

COMMENTARY: If you are not attached to anything, then you are free. If you hold something you are hindered. When you see, when you hear, and when you smell, you are never separate from the universe. But when thinking appears, then everything falls away and becomes separated. So when you are hungry, eat; when you are tired, sleep. Then you are already better then Buddhas and Bodhisattvas.

52. *Big Bell Ceremony*

One day at Su Dok Sah Temple they were having a grand ceremony to dedicate the big new temple bell. Zen Master Hae Am stepped up to give the Dharma speech, saying, "We now have a big bell. Is this bell outside or inside your mind? When you hear the bell, stand up. When you hear the drum, fall down. What does this mean?"

No one answered. Then he said, "I will give you the answer." He clenched his hand in a fist and held it up. "If this is correct . . ." opening his hand, "then this is not correct."

1. *Is this bell outside or inside your mind?*
2. *"When you hear the bell, stand up. When you hear the drum, fall down." What does this mean?*
3. *Zen Master Hae Am clenched his hand in a fist and held it up. "If this is correct . . ." opening his hand, "then this is not correct." What does this mean?*

COMMENTARY: Zen Master Hae Am was very clever and very stupid. He opened his mouth, and it was already a mistake. The stone girl hit him thirty times. Do you know the true meaning of this? When Hae Am gave his Dharma speech all the Buddhas and Bodhisattvas faced west and said, "Great Zen Master is in front of you at this moment."

53. Straight Line in the Circle

The great layman Hwa Ryon Gosa received *inga* from Zen Master Ko Bong.* One day, a student asked him, "What is Dharma?"

He answered by making a circle in the air.

The student said, "I still don't understand."

Hwa Ryon Gosa replied, "In the circle there is one place where these is a straight line, not curved. Where is that place?" The student still could not understand, so Hwa Ryon Gosa told him, "You must sit more."

1. *Hwa Ryon Gosa made a circle in the air. What does this mean?*
2. *In the circle, where is the straight line?*

COMMENTARY: The earth goes around the sun; the moon goes around the earth. They never stop, and they never go straight. But these things originally have no name and no form, and they are unmoving. When mind appears, everything appears; when mind disappears, everything disappears. When mind does not appear or disappear, then what? Then everything is straight.

Inga signifies a Zen master's "seal" or approval of a student to teach kong-an practice.

54. Before the Donkey Has Left, the Horse Has Already Arrived

A long time ago, Mun Ik asked Manjushri Bodhisattva, "How many students do you have?"

"In front three, three, in back three, three," Manjushri replied.

Zen Master Hae Am's commentary was:

> Before the donkey has left,
> the horse has already arrived.

1. *What is the meaning of "In front three, three, in back three, three"?*
2. *"Before the donkey has left, the horse has already arrived." What does this mean?*
3. *Hae Am's commentary is like scratching his right foot when his left foot itches. How can you make it correct?*

COMMENTARY: In the sky, there are many stars and moons and suns. On the ground there are many mountains, rivers, oceans, and houses. How many are there? If you understand, you become Buddha. Zen Master Hae Am had a big mouth and said, "Before the donkey has left, the horse has already arrived." But Hae Am had no mouth, so how could he say that? Silence is better than holiness.

55. Sword Mountain

Young Master So Sahn visited old Zen Master Tu Ja, who asked him, "Where are you coming from?"

So Sahn answered, "From Sword Mountain."

"Then did you bring your sword?"

"Yes, I did."

"Then show it to this old monk." So Sahn pointed one finger to the ground in front of Tu Ja, who abruptly stood up and left the room.

Later that afternoon, Tu Ja asked his attendant to invite So Sahn to have a cup of tea with him. The attendant told him that after the morning's event, So Sahn had left immediately.

Tu Ja then sang a *gatha*:

> "For 30 years I have ridden horseback,
> And today I was kicked from the horse by a
> small donkey."

1. *When the old monk asked, "Did you bring your sword?" the young monk pointed to the ground. If you were the old monk, what could you do?*
2. *So Sahn pointed to the ground. What does this mean?*
3. *"Today I was kicked from the horse by a small donkey." What does this mean?*

COMMENTARY: Beware of this donkey. If you open your mouth, then the donkey has already kicked you. If you close your mouth, then he has also kicked you. What can you do?

The donkey already kicked Master So Sahn. Tu Ja was already on horseback. But this donkey kicked both monks out of this world. How can they find their bodies? All that appears is sound, "Aigo, aigo, aigo!"

56. Give Me a Don't-Know Sentence

Once, when Zen Master Man Gong was staying at Jeong Hae Sah Temple, a student came to his room, bowed, and said, "Zen Master, since I came to this temple, I have understood many things. So today, I ask you to give me a don't-know sentence."

Without a moment's hesitation, Man Gong thrust his fist to within a half inch of the student's face. The student gasped and instantly attained enlightenment. He bowed deeply and said, "Thank you for your teaching."

1. *What did the student attain?*
2. *Give me a don't-know sentence.*
3. *Man Gong punched his fist to within a half inch of the student's face. What does this mean?*

COMMENTARY: Socrates used to walk through the streets and markets of Athens, telling people as he passed, "You must understand your true self, you must understand your true self." One of his students asked him, "Teacher, do you understand your true self?" "I don't know," he replied, "but I understand this don't-know." Man Gong's action and Socrates' action, are they the same or different? If you attain that, then you attain your true self. If you don't understand, go to the kitchen and drink cold water.

57. Zen Teachings and Sutra Teachings

Someone asked Zen Master Pa Ling, "Are Zen teachings and Sutra teachings the same or different?"

Pa Ling replied, "When a chicken is cold, it goes into a tree. When a duck is cold, it goes under water."

Zen Master Hae Am's commentary on this is, "Even though water is flowing, sound cannot be seen."

1. *Are Zen teachings and Sutra teachings the same or different?*
2. *"When a chicken is cold, it goes into a tree. When a duck is cold, it goes under water." What does this mean?*
3. *"Even though water is flowing, sound cannot be seen." What does this mean?*

COMMENTARY: The ten thousand dharmas return to the One. Where does the One return to? If you attain that point, then is that Sutra or Zen teaching? If you say "Zen," you have already received thirty blows. If you say "Sutra," then you have also received thirty blows. What can you do? Tell me, tell me! If you don't understand, go drink tea.

58. True Nature Does Not Exist

Manjushri Bodhisattva sent a poem to Precepts Master Chan Jang:

> "When you understand all
> Dharmas,
> True nature does not exist.
> Understand that Dharma nature
> Is just like this.
> Then you see Nosahna* Buddha."

In this poem there is one word which is beyond life and death, beyond mind and Buddha, so it is freedom from life and death.

1. *"True Nature does not exist." What does this mean?*
2. *"Dharma nature is just like this." What does this mean?*
3. *Which word is freedom from life and death?*

COMMENTARY: When the wind blows from the east, the clouds move west. When the wind blows from the west, the clouds move east. No wind, no clouds, no moon, no sun. Then what? See this, become Buddha.

---

*Highest Buddha.

59. *Speech, Silence, Moving, Quiet*

One day Zen Master Man Gong and Zen Master Yong Song were standing together at Son Ha Won Temple in Seoul.

Yong Song asked Man Gong, "Give me a sentence without speech, silence, moving or quiet."

Man Gong acted as if he hadn't heard.

"Isn't that silence?" Yong Song asked.

"No."

The other people there could not understand who was correct. Later, Zen Master Jun Kang heard of this exchange and said, "It is as though both masters fell into muddy water while fighting with each other."

Hae Am commented, "If someone asked me for one sentence without speech, silence, moving or quiet, I would say: 'A broken bowl cannot be put back into its original condition.' "

1. *What is silence?*
2. *Someone asks you, "Give me one sentence without speech, silence, moving or quiet." What can you do?*
3. *Zen Master Man Gong said, "No." What does this mean?*
4. *Zen Master Jun Kang said, "It is as though both masters fell into muddy water while fighting with each other." What does this mean?*
5. *Zen Master Hae Am said, "If someone asked me for one sentence without speech, silence, moving or quiet, I would say: 'A broken bowl cannot be put back into its original condition.' " What does this mean?*

COMMENTARY: All the Zen Masters are wrestling together in the mud. Where are their eyes, noses, mouths, hands and legs? Which one is Man Gong? Which one is Yong Song? Which is Jun Kang? Hae Am? They cannot be distinguished. Who made a mistake?

The sky never says, "I am the sky." The tree never says, "I am a tree." The dog only barks, "Woof, woof." If you open your mouth, you get thirty blows; if you close your mouth, then you also get thirty blows. What can you do? Put it all down. If you are thirsty, go drink some cold water.

60. The True Meaning of the Cypress Tree in the Garden

A long time ago in China, someone asked Zen Master Joju, "Why did Bodhidharma come to China?" "The cypress tree in the garden," he replied. Years later, Zen Master Song Sang commented:

"Fish moving, water becomes cloudy.
Bird flies, a feather falls."

Many Zen Masters have offered commentaries on Song Sang's verse. Zen Master Hae Am commented:

"Self-nature is already clear.
Mind moving is already a big mistake."

1. *Joju said, "The cypress tree in the garden." What does this mean?*
2. *Song Sang said, "Fish moving, water becomes cloudy. Bird flies, a feather falls." Where is his mistake? Where is there not a mistake?*
3. *"Self-nature is already clear. Mind moving is already a big mistake." That is only an explanation. What is the true meaning?*

COMMENTARY: Zen Masters Hae Am and Song Sang are wrestling with each other. They hit and kick each other. Blood is flowing; their faces are broken and bruised. But they still don't understand why they are wrestling. The cypress tree is clearly in front of you in the garden.

So why are they wrestling together? They have no eyes and no consciousness. In the clear mirror, red comes – red is reflected; white comes – white. Don't make anything. Just see

it, just do it. This is better than opening your mouth. Watch
your step!

61. *Ten Sicknesses*

When Zen Master Yong Song was staying at
Man Wol Sah Temple, he sent a letter to several
other temples in Korea which said, "In the 'Mu'
kong-an, there are ten sicknesses. Please send
me one sentence without the ten sicknesses."

Zen Master Man Gong answered, "A monk asked Zen
Master Joju, 'Does a dog have Buddha-nature?' Joju said, 'Mu.'
Yong Song replied to Man Gong, "An iron hammer without a
hole."

Zen Master Hae Am answered, "Already fell down. What
can you do?"

Zen Master Hae Wol answered, "KATZ! Is that correct or
not?"

Zen Master Song Wol wrote from Kun Jung Mountain, "On
top of Man Wol Mountain [where Yong Song was] is a cloud.
Under Kun Jung Mountain is a thief."

1. *Joju said, "Mu." What does this mean?*
2. *Where are the "Mu" kong-an's ten sicknesses?*
3. *Give me one sentence without the ten sicknesses.*

COMMENTARY: On the mountain there are many trees, in
the ocean there are many fish. They all have different names
and forms, but everything returns to one point. What is that? If
you find this one point then this kong-an is no problem. In the
clear mirror, red comes – red is reflected; white comes – white.
If you are not holding anything and not checking anything,
then your mind is clear like space. If you're thinking and
checking, then this kong-an is a thousand miles away. Be
careful!

62. The Burning Fire

You are the burning fire,
I the reflected glow.
How could I without you
and you without me grow?

1. *Who are you?*
2. *What does "I the reflected glow" mean?*
3. *"You without me grow." What does this mean?*
4. *You and me, are they the same or different?*

COMMENTARY: Mind appears, you and I are separate. Mind disappears, you and I are never separate.

63. All As Nothingness

Who sees the All as nothingness,
as nothing all that is,
sees everything through God's own eye.
Enlightenment is this.

1. *You are nothingness. So how do you see nothingness?*
2. *What is the meaning of "God's own eye"?*
3. *What does enlightenment mean?*

COMMENTARY: Open your mouth and everything appears. Close your mouth, nothing appears. So stillness is better than bliss. But be careful! Don't be attached to emptiness and stillness.

64. Pure Emptiness

The God who is pure emptiness
is created as form,
becoming substance, light and darkness,
the stillness and the storm.

1. *What is the meaning of "pure emptiness"?*
2. *What is the meaning of "becoming substance"?*

COMMENTARY: KATZ! Is that God or is that substance? If you say substance, you go to hell; if you say form you are already dead.

65. The Deepest Well

You are the deepest well
from which all rises, grows.
You are the boundless ocean
back into which all flows.

1. *What does "the deepest well" mean?*
2. *What does "boundless ocean" mean?*

COMMENTARY: How wide is your mind? How deep? If you understand this, you meet God face-to-face.

66. God Inside God

I was God inside God
before this timebound ME,
and shall be God again
When from my ME set free.

1. *"I was God inside God." What does this mean?*
2. *When will your ME be set free?*

COMMENTARY: God made everything, so everything has God-nature. If mind appears, you lose God-nature. But if you take away mind, you are always sitting with God.

67. *Empty Becoming*

The emptier I do become,
the more delivered from the Me,
the better shall I understand
what is God's liberty.

1. *If you are empty, how do you "become"?*
2. *How do you understand "God's liberty"?*

COMMENTARY: One mind has never appeared. God and you are never separate. When your mind appears, you must believe in God one hundred percent.

68. *No True One Is Elated*

By honors and by titles
no true one is elated.
To realize that which we are,
for this we were created.

1. *"No true one is elated." What does this mean?*
2. *Why were we created?*

COMMENTARY: The sun, the moon, the stars – where do they come from? If you attain this point, you can see God's face.

69. Jesus Christ

However well of Jesus Christ
you talk and sermons preach,
unless he lives within yourself,
he is beyond your reach.

1. *Who is Jesus Christ?*
2. *How does he live within you?*
3. *How do you reach him?*

COMMENTARY: The Cross sets you free. If you attain the Cross, you sit together with God.

70. Without a Single Law

The precepts are only for the wicked.
Without a single law,
the just will love all living things,
holding God's life in awe.

1. *"The just will love all living things." What does this mean?*
2. *How do you hold God's life in awe?*

COMMENTARY: The sky is blue, the water is flowing. If you attain the true meaning of this, God smiles on you.

71. The Nightingale and the Cuckoo

The Nightingale does not resent
the Cuckoo's simple song.
But you, if I don't sing like you,
tell me that I am wrong.

1. *What does "The Nightingale does not resent" mean?*
2. *What is the meaning of "The Cuckoo's simple song?"*

COMMENTARY: Dog barking, "Woof, woof!" Chicken crowing, "Cock-a-doodle-doo!"

72. Inside, Outside

If you go out, God will come in.
So die – in God withdraw.
Not-being, you will be in God,
not-doing, you will live God's law.

1. *Who makes inside and outside?*
2. *Is God inside or outside your mind?*
3. *What is "not-being"?*
4. *What is "not-doing"?*

COMMENTARY: Coming or going, God is never separate from you. If you laugh, God is happy; if you cry, God is sad.

73. Christ's Birth and Death

Christ was born human for me
and for me he died.
If I don't get transformed in God
His birth is mocked, His death denied.

1. *Does Christ have life and death?*
2. *Before Christ was born, who took care of you?*

COMMENTARY: The blue sky is Christ's face. The blue mountain is His body.

74. The Rose Blooms

The rose blooms because she blooms,
she never asks WHY?

Nor does she preen herself
to catch my wandering eye.

1. *Why does the rose bloom?*
2. *How does the rose catch your wandering eye?*

COMMENTARY: The child wants to catch the butterfly. The fisherman sinks his bait into the water.

75. *The Nature of All Things*

If to the nature of all things
you wish to penetrate,
You will know all, if you can find
the door to just one thing.

1. *How do you penetrate all things?*
2. *Where is the door to just one thing?*

COMMENTARY: Your face cannot see your face. Nature cannot see nature. If you want to see your face, it's already a big mistake; nature understanding nature is also a big mistake. How do you see your face? How do you understand nature? Be careful, be careful! Dog laughing outside, "Woof, woof!"

76. *Achievements Perish*

All you achieved and stored in barns
must perish in the end.
Therefore, become that which you are
and which the world transcends.

1. *If everything perishes in the end, where do you stay?*
2. *What does "the world transcends" mean?*

COMMENTARY: What you see now, is that God? What you hear now, is that God? If you attain this point, you will become free.

77. No Fear of Death

The wise have no fear of death,
too often they have died
to Ego and its vanities,
to all that keeps them tied.

1. *When you die, where do you go?*
2. *If you are not tied to anything, then what?*

COMMENTARY: You must pay for the rental car when you return it.

78. Always in Paradise

No thought for the hereafter
is cherished by the wise.
For on this earth they truly live
always in paradise.

1. *How do you not think about the hereafter?*
2. *What is the meaning of "always in paradise"?*

COMMENTARY: When desire appears, hell and paradise appear. When desire disappears, hell and paradise disappear.

79. The Deepest Prayer

The deepest prayer on this earth
that anyone could say
is that which makes me wholly One
with that to which I pray.

1. *When praying, how do you become one with prayer?*
2. *What is the deepest prayer?*

COMMENTARY: The mother rubs her child's stomach. The priest prays in church.

80. At the Soul's Center

Unless you find the paradise
at your soul's very center,
you haven't got the smallest chance
that you can once there enter.

1. *Where is the soul's center?*
2. *How do you enter paradise?*

COMMENTARY: Originally, there is no name and no form, so where is south, east, west, and north? If you attain this point, you attain the standing place.

81. Redemption

Christians are foolish thinking
they can attain redemption
while with their bodies and their souls
remain attached to worldly goals.

1. *How can you attain redemption?*
2. *How do you take away attachment to worldly goals?*

COMMENTARY: Don't make anything, don't want anything, and then the universe will give you everything.

82. Old Clothes

One day Zen Master Hyang Gok put on very old, tattered clothes and visited several temples. At one temple, Zen Master Ko Bong saw him and asked, "How can you fix those old clothes?"

1. *If you were Hyang Gok, how would you answer?*
2. *How much do Hyang Gok's old clothes weigh?*

COMMENTARY: In winter, you must use heavy winter clothes. In summer, use light summer clothes.

83. *The Meaning of Am Du's Whispering**

When Zen Master Hyang Gok visited Zen Master Jun Kang at Dae Gak Sah Temple, he asked Jun Kang, "What is the meaning of Am Du's whispering in the master's ear?"

"Even the Buddha and the Bodhisattvas do not understand," Jun Kang replied. "How can I understand?"

Hyang Gok cried out and left.

Then Jun Kang called out to him, "If you do not believe me, I will give you another answer."

Hyang Gok said, "I don't give acupuncture to a dead cow," and continued on his way.

Sometime later, Hyang Gok's student, Jin Jae Sunim, heard about this exchange and commented. "Ma Jo killed everybody. Lin Chi is not yet stupid."

1. *Hyang Gok cried out and left. What does this mean?*
2. *"I don't give acupuncture to a dead cow." What does this mean?*
3. *Jin Jae answered, "Ma Jo killed everybody. Lin Chi is not yet stupid." Is this correct or not?*

COMMENTARY: Three people fight in a muddy place, hit each other, and become dirty.

---

*See kong-an 292, "Dok Sahn Carrying His Bowls."

84. Whose Song Do You Sing?

One day, Jin Jae Sunim asked his teacher, Zen Master Hyang Gok, "Whose song do you sing? Whose lineage do you follow?"

Hyang Gok replied, "I received one word from Zen Master Un Mun and I have never exhausted it."

1. *Whose song do you sing?*
2. *Whose lineage do you follow?*
3. *Is Hyang Gok's answer correct or not?*

COMMENTARY: The sky is clear: Why is there lightning?

85. Money to Spend

Jin Jae Sunim persisted, "Only that? Not more?"

Zen Master Hyang Gok answered, "In my pocket I have a lot of money. In heaven and on earth, coming or going, I am free to spend it."

1. *If you were Hyang Gok, how would you answer?*
2. *Is Hyang Gok's answer correct or not?*
3. *Hyang Gok said, "In my pocket I have a lot of money." What kind of money did Hyang Gok have?*

COMMENTARY: Hyang Gok has a hole in his pocket, so he loses all his money.

86. What Is Your True Speech?

Jin Jae Sunim asked Zen Master Hyang Gok, "What is your true speech?"

Zen Master Hyang Gok said, "The cry of a mad cow appeared. Heaven and earth are surprised. The Buddha and all eminent teachers are all dead."

1. What is your true speech?
2. Is Zen Master Hyang Gok's speech true?
3. Did you hear the cry of the mad cow?

COMMENTARY: In last night's dream, a gold cow was riding in a chariot. The gold cow said, "Woof, woof!"

87. When One Is Picked Up, Seven Are Gotten

Jin Jae Sunim asked Zen Master Hyang Gok, "What is your special technique?"

Hyang Gok answered, "When one is picked up, seven are gotten."

1. What is your special technique?
2. What is the meaning of "When one is picked up, seven are gotten"?
3. One and seven come from where?

COMMENTARY: Facing the ground, pick up the moon.

88. First Word

Jin Jae Sunim asked Zen Master Hyang Gok, "What is the first word?"

Hyang Gok answered, "Shakyamuni Buddha and Maitreya Bodhisattva fell into quicksand."

1. What is the first word?
2. What is the meaning of "Shakyamuni Buddha and Maitreya Bodhisattva fell into quicksand"?
3. Is Hyang Gok's answer correct or not?

COMMENTARY: Opening your mouth is a mistake as big as Sumi Mountain. Close your mouth, you're already in hell.

89. Last Word

Jin Jae Sunim asked Zen Master Hyang Gok, "What is the last word?"

Zen Master Hyang Gok said, "In the lightning, tripped and fell down."

1. *What is the last word?*
2. *"In the lightning, tripped and fell down." What does this mean?*

COMMENTARY: Head is facing the sky, legs are pointing toward the ground.

90. Tathagata Zen

Jin Jae Sunim asked Zen Master Hyang Gok, "What is Tathagata Zen?"

Hyang Gok answered, "Keen-eyed students fall into the well."

1. *What is Tathagata Zen?*
2. *Is Hyang Gok's answer correct or not?*
3. *If you are a keen-eyed student, how do you fall into the well?*

COMMENTARY: Two legs, two hands, one head.

91. Going-Up Sentence

Jin Jae Sunim asked Zen Master Hyang Gok, "What is a 'going-up' sentence?"

Hyang Gok answered, "The Buddha and all eminent teachers fell into the fire."

1. *What is a "going-up" sentence?*
2. *Is Hyang Gok's answer correct or not?*

COMMENTARY: Cloud floating in the sky, water flowing underground.

92. Coming-Down Sentence

Jin Jae Sunim asked Zen Master Hyang Gok, "What is a 'coming-down' sentence?"

Hyang Gok said, "A stone man rides an iron cow past a jeweled world."

1. *What is a "coming-down" sentence?*
2. *What does Hyang Gok's answer mean?*
3. *Is Hyang Gok's answer correct? If not, how do you make it correct?*

COMMENTARY: In last night's dream, the stone girl got lots of money and built a temple.

93. Changing-Body Sentence

Jin Jae Sunim asked Zen Master Hyang Gok, "What is a changing-body sentence?"

Hyang Gok answered, "Three heads and six arms, swallowing and spitting freely."

1. *What is a "changing-body" sentence?*
2. *"Three heads and six arms, swallowing and spitting freely." What does this mean?*
3. *How many percent correct is Hyang Gok's answer?*

COMMENTARY: In the sky, clouds change into rain that falls down to the ground.

94. How Do You Catch the Sound of a Cicada?

One day, Zen Master Man Gong and some of his students were eating watermelon at Po Dok Sah Temple. Man Gong said, "If you can bring me the sound of a cicada, this watermelon is free. If you cannot, you must pay for it."

One monk made a sound with his mouth. One monk made a circle on the ground and, sitting in the center, said, "In form no Buddha, in Buddha no form." Another monk pretended to move like a cicada. The monks gave many different answers, but Man Gong only said, "No! No! NO!!!"

Finally, Bo Wol Sunim answered correctly. Man Gong smiled happily and said, "You understand my mind."

1. If you were there, what could you do?
2. What was Bo Wol Sunim's answer?

COMMENTARY: Hear sound, become deaf. Open your mouth, become mute. When seeing, become blind.

95. Tail of a Golden Fish

While staying at Dae Sung Sah Temple, Zen Master Kum Bong sent a letter to Zen Master Man Gong which said, "I want to fish for a golden fish's tail. Do you approve?"

Man Gong sent a letter back saying, "It's okay if you catch the tail of a golden fish, but can you eat it?"

1. What is the meaning of catching a golden fish's tail?
2. If Man Gong asked you, "Can you eat it," what could you do?

COMMENTARY: Beware, beware! A golden fish already ate up two masters.

96. Right in Front of You

One day a student asked Zen Master Man Gong, "Where is the Buddha's Dharma?"

"Right in front of you."

The student replied, "You say, 'In front of you,' but I cannot see it."

"You have 'I,' so you cannot see."

"Do you see?" the student asked.

Man Gong answered, "If you make 'I,' you cannot see. But if you make 'you,' it is even more difficult to see."

"If I have no 'I,' no 'you,' then who is speaking?"

The student was instantly enlightened.

1. What does "right in front of you" mean?
2. No "I," no "you." How do you see?
3. What did the student attain?

COMMENTARY: Stupid, stupid, stupid like a rockhead! You must see clearly, hear clearly.

97. Tea Cup

One day Man Gong Sunim was drinking tea with Zen Master Su Wol. In the middle of their conversation, Su Wol picked up a tea cup and said, "Don't say this is a tea cup. Don't say this is not a tea cup. What can you say?" Man Gong answered correctly, so Su Wol was very happy.

1. If you were there, what could you answer?

COMMENTARY: A monk likes noodles and cake. Laypeople like beautiful clothes and shoes.

98. Crying in Front of the Gate

Zen Master Hae Bong visited Zen Master Man Gong and, standing in front of the gate, cried three times, "Aigo! Aigo! Aigo!" Man Gong got up from his cushion, lay down on his bed, and correctly answered him. Then Hae Bong clapped his hands and laughed, "Ha! Ha! Ha!" Upon hearing this, Man Gong instantly got out of bed and answered him again.

1. *What was Man Gong's first answer?*
2. *What was Man Gong's second answer?*

COMMENTARY: Man Gong and Hae Bong fall together into the ocean upside down.

99. Throwing Rocks

One day, Zen Master Man Gong San visited Zen Master Hahn Am at Oh Dae Mountain's Stillness Palace Temple. When it was time for Man Gong to leave, they crossed a bridge together. Man Gong picked up a rock and threw it in front of Hahn Am, whereupon Hahn Am picked up a rock and threw it into the water.

"On this trip, much was lost," Man Gong said to himself.

1. *If you had been there, what could you have done?*
2. *Zen Master Hahn Am threw a rock into the water. What does this mean?*
3. *Man Gong said, "On this trip, much was lost." What does this mean?*

COMMENTARY: Don't make anything. Don't hold anything. Then, when you see, when you hear – that is better than Buddha.

100. No Mind, No Dharma

Zen Master Chun Song hit his Zen stick three times and said, "Even if you have Dharma, you must take it away. Why make new Dharma? Where does it come from? It comes from your mind. When mind appears, everything appears. When mind disappears, everything disappears. Where can you find Dharma? But if you have no Dharma, then you have no mind, so how can you save all beings?

"Lin Chi's 'KATZ,' Dok Sahn's hit, Guji's one finger – are they Dharma or are they mind? If you say mind, you are already dead. With no Dharma and no mind, how can you save all beings?"

After a moment of silence he hit the table and said, "When the stone girl has a baby, then you will understand."

1. *No mind, no Dharma. How can you save all beings?*
2. *Dok Sahn's hit, Lin Chi's "KATZ," and Guji's one finger – are they Dharma or mind?*
3. *What do you attain when the stone girl has a baby?*

COMMENTARY: Wonderful, wonderful! What a great man! His mind and speech are straight.

101. An Old Loan

Zen Master Man Gong sent a letter to Zen Master Hahn Am. "We have not seen each other in ten years," he wrote. "The clouds, the full moon, the mountain, and the water everywhere are the same, but I think about you staying in the cold north and wish you would bring your bag south where it is warm, and teach students here."

Hahn Am wrote back, "I am very poor. I think about an old loan."

Man Gong answered, "The old man loved his grandson and his mouth is poor."

Hahn Am wrote, "The thief has already passed. Don't pull your bow."

Man Gong replied, "The arrow has already pierced the thief's head."

What is the meaning of:
1. *"I am very poor. I think about an old loan."*
2. *"The old man loved his grandson and his mouth is poor."*
3. *"The thief has already passed. Don't pull your bow."*
4. *"The arrow has already pierced the thief's head."*

COMMENTARY: Two old men pulling the arms of a young child, shouting, "That's my son!" "No, that's *my* son!" Letting go is better than holding.

102. The Great Way Has No Gate

A monk asked Zen Master Hyang Gok, "What is the meaning of 'The great way has no gate'?"

Hyang Gok replied, "Quiet, quiet speech."

The monk asked, "What is quiet, quiet speech?"

"East, west, ten million worlds. South, north, one million lands."

1. *What is the meaning of "The great way has no gate"?*
2. *What is "quiet, quiet speech"?*
3. *Are Hyang Gok's two answers correct or not?*

COMMENTARY: Opening your mouth is already a mistake: You must use your legs.

103. Joju's Cypress Tree in the Garden

A monk asked Zen Master Hyang Gok, "What is the meaning of Joju's cypress tree in the garden?"

"Living in a strong tiger's mouth, falling into a blue dragon's cave."

1. *What does Joju's cypress tree in the garden mean?*
2. *What does Hyang Gok's answer mean?*
3. *Can you live in a tiger's mouth?*

COMMENTARY: Look! Look at the cypress tree in the garden. Then you will get it.

104. The Meaning of Joju's "Mu"

A monk asked, "What is the meaning of Joju's 'Mu'?"

Hyang Gok answered, "A demon falls down. Buddha runs away, scared and shaking."

1. *What does "Mu" mean?*
2. *"A demon falls down. Buddha runs away, scared and shaking." What does this mean?*

COMMENTARY: You must visit a dairy farm and listen carefully to the cow's song.

105. The Meaning of Dry Shit on a Stick

A monk asked Zen Master Hyang Gok, "What does Un Mun's 'Dry shit on a stick' mean?"

Hyang Gok answered, "The bright sun appears in the sky at midnight. Above heaven, below heaven, without equal."

1. What does Un Mun's "Dry shit on a stick" mean?
2. Is Hyang Gok's answer correct?
3. Did you see the bright sun appear in the sky at midnight?

COMMENTARY: You must go to a farm and ask the farmer, "Where's the dry shit on a stick?"

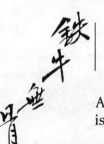

106. The Meaning of Three Pounds of Flax

A monk asked Zen Master Hyang Gok, "What is the meaning of 'three pounds of flax'?"

"The iron cow was surprised, ran away past the western sky and Sumi Mountain, then crossed the big river at midnight."

1. What is the meaning of "Three pounds of flax"?
2. How many percent correct is Hyang Gok's answer?
3. "The iron cow . . . crossed the big river at midnight." What does this mean?

COMMENTARY: Wake up! See clearly, hear clearly. One pound of iron equals one pound of kapok.

107. Realm of Enlightenment

A monk asked Zen Master Hyang Gok, "What is your realm of enlightenment?"

"Sun rising, Manjushri's house. Moon setting, Kwan Seum Bosal's house."

1. What is your realm of enlightenment?
2. Manjushri's house and Kwan Seum Bosal's house, are they the same or different?

COMMENTARY: In the morning, the sun rises in the east. In the evening, the sun sets in the west.

108. What Is Your Everyday Life?

When a monk asked Zen Master Hyang Gok, "What is your everyday life?" Hyang Gok answered, "Break the blue dragon's cave with an iron hammer. Change a golden-haired lion into a dog."

1. What is your everyday life?
2. Is Hyang Gok's answer correct or not?
3. How do you break the blue dragon's cave and change the golden-haired lion into a dog?

COMMENTARY: When you are tired, sleep. When you are hungry, eat. When you meet someone, just ask, "How are you today?"

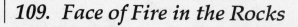

109. *Face of Fire in the Rocks*

When someone asked Zen Master Hyang Gok, "What is Buddha?" he answered, "Face of fire in the rocks."

1. *What is Buddha?*
2. *What is the meaning of "Face of fire in the rocks"?*

COMMENTARY: The train goes down the tracks. The bus goes down the highway.

110. *Face of Rocks in the Fire*

When someone asked Zen Master Hyang Gok, "What is the eminent teacher?" he answered, "Face of rocks in the fire."

1. *What is the eminent teacher?*
2. *What is the meaning of "Face of rocks in the fire"?*

COMMENTARY: Hyang Gok's face is in heaven and his body is in hell.

111. *Hyang Gok's "Bodhidharma's Coming to China"*

When someone asked Zen Master Hyang Gok, "What is the meaning of Bodhidharma's coming to China?" he answered, "Make a mad horse in the fire."

1. *What is the meaning of Bodhidharma's coming to China?*
2. *How do you make a mad horse in the fire?*

COMMENTARY: Bodhidharma had two eyes, two ears and one mouth. Three years after he died he was alive again. See his body clearly. Hear his sound clearly.

112. Where All Buddhas Appear

Someone asked Zen Master Hyang Gok, "What is the place where all Buddhas appear?"

"Iron cow runs over a bridge of rabbit's horn," he responded.

1. *What is the place were all Buddhas appear?*
2. *Did you see the rabbit's horn and the iron cow running?*

COMMENTARY: See clearly, hear clearly. Water is flowing, the wind is blowing.

113. What Is Meditation?

Someone asked Zen Master Hyang Gok, "What is meditation?"

"Not-moving form in the morning," he replied.

1. *What is meditation?*
2. *What is "not-moving form in the morning"?*

COMMENTARY: Open your mouth and you will receive thirty blows.

114. Great Liberation

Someone asked Zen Master Hyang Gok, "What is great liberation?"

"Mad cow crossed a big river."

1. *What is great liberation?*
2. *How does a mad cow cross a big river?*

COMMENTARY: If you are moving, you are already dead. If you are not moving, you instantly fall into the river of hell.

115. The Samadhi of Great Stillness

Someone asked Zen Master Hyang Gok, "What is the samadhi of great stillness?"

"A long time ago the golden bird flew into the North Star and still received no news," he replied.

1. *What is the samadhi of great stillness?*
2. *What is the meaning of "no news"?*

COMMENTARY: Opening your mouth, you lose your tongue.

116. Clear Original Body

Once a student asked Zen Master Hyang Gok, "What is the clear original body?"

"The treasure sword is hidden in the Diamond Eyes," he answered.

1. *What is the clear original body?*
2. *What is the meaning of "The treasure sword is hidden in the Diamond Eyes"?*
3. *What is the treasure sword?*

COMMENTARY: In the morning, eat breakfast. At noon, eat lunch.

117. Pomegranate Feast

Bo Wol offered a ripe pomegranate to Zen Master Man Gong. As he was handing it to his teacher, he said, "Please eat this fruit in a feast with the Bodhisattvas of the ten directions and the Buddhas of the three worlds." Man Gong took the fruit, ate it, and smiled. "How is it?" Bo Wol asked.

"The Bodhisattvas of the ten directions and the Buddhas of the three worlds have already finished the feast," Man Gong replied.

1. *The Bodhisattvas of the ten directions and the Buddhas of the three worlds come from where?*
2. *How did Zen Master Man Gong feast with Bodhisattvas?*

COMMENTARY: Monkeys like bananas. Horses like apples.

118. Stone Kwan Seum Bosal

Zen Master Man Gong, while standing in front of the stone Kwan Seum Bosal statue at Jeong Hae Sah Temple, said to his student, Bo Wol, "Describe Kwan Seum Bosal's face."

"Beneficent," was the reply. Upon hearing this, Man Gong returned to his room.

1. *If you were Bo Wol, how would you answer?*
2. *Man Gong said nothing and returned to his room. What is the meaning of this action?*

3. *If you were Man Gong and Bo Wol gave you this answer, what would you do?*
4. *Who was the winner and who was the loser?*

COMMENTARY: Man Gong and Bo Wol are wrestling in a mud puddle. Who wins, who loses? The statue has a mouth but no speech. It has eyes but cannot see. When you hear the statue's speech, and the statue sees, then you are complete.

119. In the Sound of the Bell, Attain Enlightenment

Zen Master Seung Sahn's grandteacher, Man Gong, gave a Dharma speech to a group of monks: "All Zen Masters say that in the sound of the bell they attain enlightenment, and at the sound of the drum they fall down. Anyone who understands the meaning of this, please give me an answer."

A student named Song Wol stood up and said, "If the rabbit's horn is correct, the sheep's horn is false." Man Gong smiled.

1. *"In the sound of the bell they attain enlightenment, and at the sound of the drum they fall down." What does this mean?*
2. *"If the rabbit's horn is correct, the sheep's horn is false." What does this mean?*
3. *Was Man Gong's smile a reward or punishment?*

COMMENTARY: If you cannot hear the bell or the drum, you are free. If you hear both sounds you are already in hell.

120. The Great Work of Life and Death

Carrying rice paper and brush, Yong Um Sunim entered Zen Master Man Gong's room and said, "Master, please write down one sentence." Man Gong took the brush and wrote, "This is the realm of finishing the great work of life and death: At midnight on the mountain peak the monkey's cry is very noisy." Yong Um thanked Man Gong and kept this sentence his whole life. Later, Zen Master Kum Bong read the sentence and said, "Zen Master Man Gong's keen eyes and bone marrow are in this sentence."

1. *What is "the realm of finishing the great work of life and death"?*
2. *"At midnight on the mountain peak the monkey's cry is very noisy." What does this mean?*
3. *What are Man Gong's keen eyes and bone marrow?*

COMMENTARY: Speech and words are free. Action is a hindrance. So your mouth and body must have a good friendship.

121. Best Killer

One day Hyo Bong Sunim asked Zen Master Man Gong, "Somebody likes to kill. Who is the best killer?"

Man Gong said, "Today I see him here."

"I want to cut your neck," Hyo Bong said. "Do you give me permission?"

Man Gong answered him. Then Hyo Bong was very happy and bowed to his teacher.

1. *Who is the best killer?*
2. *Man Gong said, "Today I see him here." What does this mean?*
3. *What was Man Gong's second answer?*

COMMENTARY: Be careful. Don't give a sharp knife to a child.

122. *Big Temple*

Zen Master Man Gong told the following story to Hyo Bong Sunim: "A long time ago, the Heaven King picked up a blade of grass and put it back into the ground. He then said to Shakyamuni Buddha, 'I made a big temple here.' The Buddha smiled.

"So, Hyo Bong Sunim, do you understand the meaning of this?"

Hyo Bong gave an answer to Zen Master Man Gong, who clapped his hands and, laughing, said, "Wonderful, wonderful!"

1. *"I have made a big temple here." What does this mean?*
2. *What does the Buddha's smile mean?*
3. *What was Hyo Bong Sunim's answer to Zen Master Man Gong?*

COMMENTARY: Everything is impermanent. Why make a temple? If you attain "Everything is impermanent," you attain the true temple.

123. *Departure Poem*

Ko Bong Sunim went into Zen Master Man Gong's room, bowed to his teacher, and said, "I will soon leave and travel around the country."

"If you are leaving, give me a departure poem," Man Gong said.

But Ko Bong only waved his hands in denial and said, "Today I am very busy. I cannot wrote a poem."

"I'll see you next time," his teacher said. "Have a good trip."

1. *If you had been there, what would your departure poem have been?*
2. *Ko Bong waved his hands and said, "Today I am very busy. I cannot make a poem." Is that reply correct?*

COMMENTARY: Already everything is very clear: staying, coming and going. A beautiful poem is already in front of you.

124. Let's Drink Tea

Ko Bong Sunim went into Zen Master Man Gong's room and bowed to him.

"Welcome, Ko Bong. Let's drink some tea."

Ko Bong then helped Man Gong, bowed, and sat down. Man Gong was very happy.

1. *Man Gong said, "Let's drink some tea." At that time, what would you have done?*
2. *How did Ko Bong help Man Gong?*

COMMENTARY: Ko Bong has two hands. Man Gong has one mouth. Already teatime and dinnertime have passed. Open the door and go downtown.

125. Does an Enlightened Person Have Life and Death?

Kum Bong asked Zen Master Hae Wol, "If a person gets enlightenment, does that person have life and death?"

Hae Wol replied, "Do you see the sky? Does it appear or disappear?" Kum Bong couldn't answer. He then went to see Zen Master Man Gong and told him of his exchange with Hae Wol.

Man Gong said, "Why did you leave Zen Master Hae Wol without answering him, and then come to me?"

"What could I have said?"

Man Gong replied, "Why do you do so much checking?" Kum Bong was stuck again. Then suddenly he attained, stood up and bowed to the Zen Master. Man Gong was very happy and said, "Wonderful, wonderful!"

1. *Does an enlightened person have life and death?*
2. *Does the sky appear or disappear?*
3. *What did Kum Bong attain?*

COMMENTARY: If you are thirsty, have a drink. If you are tired, sleep. The sky is always blue, and the mountain is forever green. The dog understands dog's job; the cat understands cat's job.

126. Wei Sahn's Cow

Zen Master Jun Kang once gave the following Dharma speech: "Everything has Buddha-nature. But Buddha-nature is originally empty. So how can everything have Buddha-nature?" The assembly of monks was silent.

He continued, "A long time ago, the famous Chinese Zen Master Wei Sahn said, 'When I die, I will be reborn a cow at my layman's house.'

"So my question is, what do you call him? Is he Wei Sahn or is he a cow?"

1. *Everything has Buddha-nature. But Buddha-nature is originally empty. So how can everything have Buddha-nature?*
2. *When Wei Sahn dies, he becomes a cow: at that time, would you call him Zen Master Wei Sahn or a cow?*

COMMENTARY: What do you see now? What do you hear now? Everything is clear in front of you.

127. Stone Buddha

Zen Master Man Gong was walking in the countryside with Sae Kyong Sunim, who saw a stone Buddha in the field and said to Man Gong, "I think that Buddha is very old. When was it made, Master?"

"Before the ancient Buddha appeared."

1. *What is stone Buddha?*
2. *"Before the ancient Buddha appeared." What does this mean?*

COMMENTARY: See clearly, hear clearly. The earth is round, the sky has no limits. If you meet a Buddha, offer incense and bow three times. If there is no Buddha, sit on the ground.

128. The Buddha's Breast

Hae Am Sunim was standing in front of a statue of the Buddha with Zen Master Man Gong, who said, "The Buddha's breast is very wonderful and big, so at this temple all the monks have enough food."

"If someone does not have good karma, how can they drink the Buddha's milk?" Hae Am asked.

Man Gong looked at Hae Am and said, "What did you say?"

"I said, 'If someone does not have good karma, how can they drink the Buddha's milk?'"

Man Gong replied, "You only touch the Buddha's breast, so you cannot drink the Buddha's milk."

1. *How do you drink the Buddha's milk?*
2. *What is good karma?*
3. *Man Gong said, "You only touch the Buddha's breast, so you cannot drink the Buddha's milk." What does this mean?*

COMMENTARY: My stomach is already full of milk. I must go to sleep.

129. Why Do You Cover Your Eyes?

One day Gum Oh Sunim visited Zen Master Man Gong. Upon entering the Master's room he said, "Nothing, nothing. Where is the great Zen Master?"

Man Gong asked, "Why do you cover your eyes?"

Again Gum Oh said, "Nothing, nothing. Where is the great Zen Master?"

Man Gong replied, "You are a liar who hangs around these parts."

Then Gum Oh said, "Master, be careful, be careful. Don't be deceived."

Man Gong smiled and laughed.

1. Gum Oh said, "Nothing, nothing. Where is the great Zen Master?" What does this mean?
2. Zen Master Man Gong replied, "Why do you cover your eyes?" What does this mean?
3. If somebody lies to you, what can you do?

COMMENTARY: Two blind men, wrestling each other, fall into the mud. How do they get out?

130. Hae Cho Asks About Buddha

Hae Cho asked Zen Master Poep An, "What is Buddha?"

"Hae Cho!"

"Yes?"

"That is Buddha," Poep An said.

1. What is Buddha?
2. Poep An said, "Hae Cho!" What does this mean?
3. Hae Cho replied, "Yes?" and Poep An said, "That is Buddha." What does this mean?

COMMENTARY: Hae Cho is Buddha, Buddha is Hae Cho. No Hae Cho, no Buddha. Hae Cho is Hae Cho, Buddha is Buddha. Which one do you like?

131. Why Bodhidharma Came to China

Dae Un Sunim said to Zen Master Man Gong: "Kwan Sahn No Sunim and I visited Zen Master Hahn Am. Kwan Sahn asked him, 'Outside, this mountain is very dry, but inside, it is not dry, so a lot of grass and trees grow on it – it is very strong. What does this mean?' Hahn Am answered by chomping his teeth together three times. I don't understand what this means, master. Please teach me."

"That has already passed," Man Gong said. "Hahn Am and Kwan Sahn No Sunim are no longer necessary. You must ask me your question."

"Why did Bodhidharma come to China?"

Man Gong replied, "A long time ago, Ananda asked Mahakashyapa, 'The Buddha transmitted to you the Golden Brocade Robe. What else did he transmit to you?' So, Mahakashyapa called out, 'Ananda!' 'Yes, sir?' 'Knock down the flagpole in front of the gate.' Dae Un Sunim, do you understand what this means? If you do, then you understand why Bodhidharma came to China."

Dae Un stood up and bowed to Man Gong, but the great Zen Master only laughed and said, "No, no. More practice is necessary."

1. *Han Am chomped his teeth together three times. What does this mean?*
2. *"Bodhidharma came to China." What does this mean?*
3. *How do you knock down the flagpole in front of the gate?*
4. *Why did Man Gong laugh and say, "No, no. More practice is necessary"?*

COMMENTARY: The American flag has many stars and stripes. The Japanese flag has a red sun. The South Korean flag has yin-yang.

132. Dragon's Nostrils

Zen Master Man Gong returned to Jeong Hae Sah from Oh Dae Sahn Stillness Palace Treasure Temple. Upon his arrival, Boek Cho Sunim asked him, "Master, at Oh Dae Sahn Stillness Palace Treasure Temple there is a dragon. Did you see the dragon's nostrils or not?"
"Yes, I saw them."
"How big are they?"
Man Gong made a "hmhhh" sound.

1. *What are dragon's nostrils?*
2. *Man Gong made a "hmhhh" sound. What does this mean?*

COMMENTARY: The dragon's breath blew Man Gong and Boek Cho to heaven.

133. Everything Has Already Become Buddha

During a Dharma speech delivered from the high rostrum, Zen Master Man Gong had the following exchange with a student: "One sutra says, 'Everything has already become Buddha.' Does anyone understand what this means?"
Jin Song Sunim answered, "Dirty water, two buckets."
Man Gong shouted, "How do you take care of dirty water?"
Jin Song shouted "KATZ!"
Man Gong hit Jin Song on the head with his Zen stick
Jin Song bowed to Man Gong and left.

Then Man Gong said, "The correct Zen Dharma eyes are not reckless."

1. *"Everything has already become Buddha." What does this mean?*
2. *Why did Jin Song say "Dirty water, two buckets"?*
3. *Where is Jin Song's mistake?*
4. *What does Man Gong's "Zen Dharma eyes are not reckless" mean?*

COMMENTARY: Grandson is crying. The grandmother is sad and gives him candy.

| 134. Candlelight

One evening, Zen Master Man Gong lit a candle by the window in his room. He then asked his attendant, "Which is the correct light, the candlelight or the light reflected in the window?"

The attendant blew out the candle and said, "Master, what can you do?" Man Gong then re-lit the candle.

1. *Man Gong asked, "Which is the correct light, the candlelight or the light reflected in the window?" If you were the attendant, how would you have answered?*
2. *Before Man Gong lit the candle, there was no light. Where did the light come from?*

COMMENTARY: No eyes, no light. No mouth, no speech. If you turn on the light, the room is bright. If you turn off the light, the room is dark.

135. Why Do You Bring Me Tea?

One day, while Zen Master Man Gong was sitting in his room and enjoying the view outside his window, his attendant brought him some tea. Man Gong said, "Every day I don't do anything. Why do you bring me tea?"

His attendant leaned close to him and said, "Have another cup, please."

Master Man Gong smiled.

1. *"Every day I don't do anything." What does this mean?*
2. *If you were the attendant, how would you have answered Man Gong?*

COMMENTARY: One mind appears, the whole world appears. One mind disappears, the whole world disappears. Don't check – just do it.

136. Your Temple Buddha Is White

One morning, during a particularly snowy winter, two nuns swept the snow from the road that ran between Kyun Song Am and Zen Master Man Gong's residence at nearby Jun Wol Sah Hermitage. When they reached his quarters, they bowed to him and said, "Master, we have removed the snow from the road. We invite you to have breakfast. Please come."

"I will not go on your clean road," he said.

One of the nuns asked, "Then what road will you take?"

"Your temple Buddha is white."

1. *Man Gong said, "I will not go on your clean road." What does this mean?*
2. *"Your temple Buddha is white." What does this mean?*

COMMENTARY: Two nuns killed Man Gong, but they still have mouths.

137. Mahakashyapa's Flag

One day Zen Master Man Gong gave a Dharma speech from the high rostrum. "Ananda asked Mahakashyapa, 'The Buddha transmitted the golden brocade robe to you. What else did he transmit to you?' Mahakashyapa called out, 'Ananda!' 'Yes, Sir!' 'Knock down the flagpole in front of the gate.' So I ask you, what else did the Buddha transmit? What is the meaning of this?"

At that time, the Head Nun Poep Hi Sunim called out, "Great Zen Master! Fish swimming, water is a little cloudy. Bird flying, feathers come off."

Then Boek Cho Sunim called out, "Zen Master! You are a great Master, so I cannot talk to you."

"Why can't you talk to me?"

"Great Master, you don't understand my speech."

Man Gong replied, "These ears are very old."

1. Ananda asked Mahakashyapa, "What else did he transmit to you?" What does this mean?
2. Poep Hi answered, "Fish swimming, water is a little cloudy. Bird flying, feathers come off." What does this mean?
3. Boek Cho said, "You are a great Master, so I cannot talk to you." What does this mean?
4. What does Boek Cho's second answer, "Great Master, you don't understand my speech," mean?
5. Man Gong replied, "These ears are very old." What does this mean?

COMMENTARY: Three people start fighting in a boat and the boat capsizes. Then they yell, "Help! Help!"

138. The Complete Stillness Jewel Palace

One day Zen Master Man Gong received a letter from Hae In Sah Temple. The monks asked, "In the ten directions, numberless temples are made in the Complete Stillness Jewel Palace. We are not clear about this. So we ask you, Master, where is the Complete Stillness Jewel Palace?"

Man Gong wrote them this poem:

In the ten directions,
numberless temples
are in the Complete Stillness Jewel Palace.
This palace is built in my nostril.

They wrote back to Man Gong and said, "You say the Complete Stillness Jewel Palace is built in your nostril. We want you to guide us to the Complete Stillness Jewel Palace."

Man Gong replied, "Why don't you know? You already stay in the Complete Stillness Jewel Palace at Hae In Sah Temple in Ka Ya Sahn."

1. *Where is the Complete Stillness Jewel Palace?*
2. *Man Gong said, "This palace is built in my nostril." What does this mean?*
3. *What Does Man Gong's second answer, "You already stay at the Complete Stillness Jewel Palace in Hae In Sah Temple in Ka Ya Sahn" mean?*

COMMENTARY: This nose comes from where? Who made this nose? Originally there is no nose. How does a temple appear?

139. The Buddha Saw a Star

星 明 看

Zen Master Man Gong received a letter on Buddha's Enlightenment Day, in which the monks of Kung Dong Zen Temple asked him,

"On December 8 in the early morning the Buddha saw a star and got Enlightenment. What does this mean?"

Man Gong wrote back, "The Buddha saw a star and said he got Enlightenment. This is sand falling into the eyes."

1. *"The Buddha saw a star and got Enlightenment." What does this mean?*
2. *What kind of star did the Buddha see when he got Enlightenment?*
3. *"This is sand falling into the eyes." What does this mean?*

COMMENTARY: Does this star come from your mind, your eyes, or the sky? If you attain this point, you attain your true self.

140. Cannot Get Out

Layman Sok Du made a circle on the ground, pointed to it and asked Zen Master Man Gong, "Master, all the great monks in the world cannot go in. Why?"

Man Gong replied, "All the great monks in the world cannot get out of it."

1. *Layman Sok Du made a circle. What does this mean?*
2. *Why can't all the great monks go into the circle?*
3. *Man Gong replied, "All the great monks in the world cannot get out of it." What does this mean?*

COMMENTARY: Don't make anything. Open your mouth and you go straight to hell like an arrow. Close your mouth and you have already lost your life. You must perceive that.

141. Rat New Year

For the Rat New Year, a layman sent a letter to Zen Master Man Gong which said, "Everybody says, 'Old year going, new year coming.' I don't

understand. Old year and new year, what does that mean?"
"This is Rat New Year," Man Gong replied.

1. *Old year going, new year coming. Coming from where? Going where?*
2. *What is old year? What is new year?*
3. *What is Rat New Year?*

COMMENTARY: The rabbit's ears are long and its tail is short.

142. *Heaven and Earth Are Separate*

When Zen Master Seung Sahn's grandteacher, Zen Master Mang Gong, was staying at Kum Sun Hermitage in Jeong Hae Sah Temple, Zen Master Hae Bong visited him and said, "There's an old saying, 'In the true, even if there is one hair's breadth, heaven and earth are separate.'"

Mang Gong replied, "Even if there is no hair's breadth, heaven and earth are separate."

1. *"Even if there is one hair's breadth, heaven and earth are separate." What does this mean?*
2. *"Even if there is not one hair's breadth, heaven and earth are separate." What does this mean?*
3. *What is the difference between one hair's breadth and not one hair's breadth?*

COMMENTARY: If you open your mouth, it's a mistake. If you keep your mouth closed, then that, too, is a mistake. Without an open or closed mouth, just see, just hear.

143. *Understand Your Job*

One day, as Zen Master Man Gong was giving a Dharma speech from the high rostrum, Zen Master Hae Bong opened the door to the room and came in. Man Gong interrupted the speech to say, "Now the great tiger is coming in."

Immediately, Hae Bong took a tiger's form and roared, "Rrrrwww!"

Man Gong said, "He understands his job. Only go straight."

1. *Why did Zen Master Man Gong say "Now the great tiger is coming in"?*
2. *Why did Zen Master Hae Bong take a tiger's form and roar?*
3. *What is your original job?*

COMMENTARY: A tiger understands a tiger. A dog understands a dog.

144. *Space Also Becomes Old*

One summertime Zen Master Man Gong visited Zen Master Yong Song in Seoul. As they sat facing each other, Yong Song said, "Man Gong, you have become old."

"Space also becomes old," Man Gong replied. "Why wouldn't this form-body become old?"

1. *No life, no death. How do you become old?*
2. *"Space also becomes old." What does this mean?*
3. *If you say Dharma-body and form-body are the same, then Dharma-body also becomes old. If you say they are different, those two bodies come from where?*

COMMENTARY: Form is emptiness, emptiness is form. No form, no emptiness. Form is form, emptiness is emptiness.

145. *Happy New Year*

While staying at Nae Jang Sah Temple, Zen Master Sol Bong sent a New Year's card to Zen Master Man Gong. In the card he asked, "How do you take one more step from the top of a hundred-foot pole?"

Man Gong answered, "KATZ! Happy New Year!"

1. *How do you take one more step from the top of a hundred-foot pole?*
2. *"KATZ! Happy New Year!" What does this mean?*

COMMENTARY: Aigo! Aigo! Aigo!

146. *Hold Up One Finger*

One day, Zen Master Sol Bong visited Kum Sun Hermitage in Jeong Hae Sah Temple and asked Zen Master Man Gong, "The Buddha held up a flower. What does this mean?"

Man Gong held up one finger.

Sol Bong bowed to him.

"What did you attain?" Man Gong asked.

Sol Bong replied, "A second offense is not permitted."

1. *The Buddha held up a flower. What does this mean?*
2. *Man Gong held up one finger. What does this mean?*
3. *What did Sol Bong attain?*
4. *Why did Sol Bong say, "A second offense is not permitted"?*

COMMENTARY: Mistake, mistake, mistake. Flower and finger are very clear. The flower is the flower, the finger is the finger.

147. *Peop Ki Bosal's Grass*

After a visit to Diamond Mountain in what is now North Korea, Zen Master Man Gong returned to Jeong Hae Sah Temple and gave a Dharma speech: "When I went to Diamond Mountain, I heard about Poep Ki Bosal, so I went to listen to her give a speech. She said, 'Students, do you understand why grass grows up three inches?'" Pausing for a moment, Man Gong asked the assembly of monks, "Do you understand the true meaning of this?" Nobody could answer him.

Later, one of the students asked Man Gong, "Poep Ki Bosal said, 'Grass grows up three inches.' What does this mean?"

Man Gong replied, "Don't ask me about grass growing up. You must go out into the grass, and then you will understand Buddha's obligation."

The student asked, "How do I go out into the grass?"

Man Gong said, "Walking at night is not permitted. Come ask me tomorrow."

1. *"Grass grows up three inches." What does this mean?*
2. *"Grass grows up" and "into the grass" — are they the same or different?*
3. *"Walking at night is not permitted. Come ask me tomorrow." What does this mean?*

COMMENTARY: Stupid, stupid, stupid. If you find Poep Ki Bosal's mouth, then you will understand.

148. *Hak Myong's Five Questions*

Zen Master Hak Myong of Nae Jang Sah Temple sent five questions to all the Zen Temples in Korea. The questions were:

1. Snow comes down and completely fills the valley. Why is there only one pine tree still standing there?

2. The whole world is Vairocana Buddha's body. Where can you find your true self?
3. The whole river flows into the ocean. Where can you taste fresh water?
4. Before becoming a cicada, broken caterpillar. At that time, not cicada, not caterpillar: What do you call it?
5. In this world, everyone has many close friends. Who is the closest?

Zen Master Man Gong answered him, "Too much thinking. I give you thirty blows. This stick – what do you call it?"

1. *How do you answer the five questions, one by one?*
2. *Man Gong said, "Too much thinking. I give you thirty blows." Is that correct or not?*
3. *Man Gong asked, "This stick – what do you call it?" So, I ask you, what do you call it?*

COMMENTARY: Five entrances into one room.

149. Three Zen Masters' "KATZ!"

One day Zen Master Hae Wol invited Zen Master Man Gong to Tong Do Sah Temple. Lunch was served and everyone was about to begin, when suddenly Hae Wol shouted "KATZ!" Everyone was very surprised, but the Head Monk simply hit the chukpi, so they all began eating. At the end of the meal, just before the chukpi was hit again, Man Gong shouted "KATZ!" Everyone was startled, but the Head Monk just hit the chukpi three times and the meal was over.

Later, monks from all the Zen temples began talking about the two Zen Masters' "KATZ": "Which one is correct?" "Are they the same or different?" "What do they mean?" Finally, one monk asked Yong Song, "What is the meaning of the two Zen Masters' 'KATZ!'?"

Yong Song replied, "I don't like to open my mouth, but because everybody wants to know what this means, I will teach you."

Then Yong Song shouted, "KATZ!"

1. *What does Hae Wol's "KATZ!" mean?*
2. *What does Man Gong's "KATZ!" mean?*
3. *Are the three Zen Masters' "KATZ!" the same or different?*

COMMENTARY: If you attain "KATZ!" you understand Man Gong's mouth and Hae Wol's ears.

150. *Mind Light*

Poem by Zen Master Kyong Ho

Moments before he died, Zen Master Kyong Ho wrote the following poem:

The mind moon is very bright and round –
Its light swallows everything.
When both mind and light disappear,
What . . . is . . . this . . . ?

1. *"The mind moon is very bright and round." What does this mean?*
2. *How can light swallow everything?*
3. *"Mind and light disappear" – then what?*

COMMENTARY: Don't make anything. What do you see now? What do you hear now? When you are doing something, just do it.

151. *The Tree with No Shadow*

Poem by Zen Master Kyong Ho

That's funny –
Riding a cow, wanting to find a cow.

When you find the tree with no shadow,
The ocean's waves all disappear.

1. *"That's funny – riding a cow, wanting to find a cow." What does this mean?*
2. *Where is the tree with no shadow?*
3. *"The ocean's waves all disappear." Then what?*

COMMENTARY: Wake up! The mountain is blue, the water is flowing – Dol, dol, dol.

152. *Zen Master Man Gong's Poem for His Teacher, Zen Master Kyong Ho**

Empty mirror is originally no mirror.
Wake-up cow, there is no cow,
No place, no road.
Open eyes: drink and sex

1. *"Originally no mirror." Then what?*
2. *"Wake up cow, there is no cow." Then what?*
3. *"No place, no road." Where do you stay?*
4. *"Open eyes: drink and sex." What does this mean?*

COMMENTARY: Everything is free: eyes, ears, nose, tongue, body, mind. That is a great man.

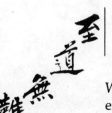

153. *Zen Master Man Gong's Enlightenment Poem*

When Zen Master Man Gong attained enlightenment, at the age of twenty-six, he composed the following poem:

---

*Kyong Ho means "empty mirror."

Empty mountain, true energy without time and
    space.
White cloud and clear wind come and go by
    themselves.
Why did Bodhidharma come to China?
Rooster crowing in the morning,
Sun rising in the east.

1. *What is the meaning of "Empty mountain, true energy
   without time and space"?*
2. *Why did Bodhidharma come to China?*
3. *Why is the chicken crowing at 3 am, the sun rising at 7 am?*

COMMENTARY: Silence is better than holiness. If you are
tired, go to your room and sleep.

154. *Zen Master Man Gong's Portrait Poem*

I never leave you,
You never leave me.
Before "you" and "I" appear,
What is this?

1. *Who is first, you or me?*
2. *Before "you" and "I" appear, what?*
3. *Is Zen Master Man Gong inside or outside his portrait?*

COMMENTARY: Before words, what is your original face?
Here is your clear mirror.

155. *Poem at Blue Ocean*

by Zen Master Man Gong

A man swallowed and spit out the whole
world.
Passing blue ocean – there hides body and
dragon's horn.
Diamond Poep Ki Bosal's body punctures the
sky.
Vast blue ocean – ancient Buddha's mind.

1. *"A man swallowed and spit out the whole world." What
does this mean?*
2. *"Vast blue ocean – ancient Buddha's mind." What does this
mean?*

COMMENTARY: Stone cat is barking; ice snake pierces the
diamond eyes.

156. *Poem for a Student, Hae Il**

by Zen Master Man Gong

Wisdom sun makes the sky become red.
Mind moon is always white.
Red and white never end.
Everything – great peace in spring.

1. *What is wisdom sun?*
2. *What is mind moon?*
3. *"Everything – great peace in spring." What does this mean?*

COMMENTARY: Spring has flowers, in winter there is snow.
The sun shines during the day, and at night the moon is
bright.

---

*Hae Il means "wisdom sun."

157. *Poem for White Cloud*

by Zen Master Man Gong

Don't say white cloud is a no-mind guest.
The old monk forgets everything.
But white cloud, why are you not my friend?
Far away a chicken is crowing, then find
    myself.

1. *"The old monk forgets everything." Then what?*
2. *Are you and the white cloud the same or different?*
3. *"Far away a chicken crowing, then find myself." What does this mean?*

COMMENTARY: The stone dog is barking. The ice fish is afraid and runs away.

158. *Poem for Pal Gong Sah Temple*

by Zen Master Man Gong

After night, rain comes.
10,000 Buddhas don't understand that.
Don't know and don't know.
When you hear the bell ring, attain go-away.

1. *"10,000 Buddhas don't understand that." What does this mean?*
2. *"Don't know and don't know." What does this mean?*
3. *"When you hear the bell ring, attain go-away." What did you attain?*

COMMENTARY: The bell rings, "Ding, ding." All the monks take their robes into the Dharma room.

159. Poem for Buddha's Enlightenment Day

by Zen Master Man Gong

The Buddha saw a star, got enlightenment.
Man Gong saw a star, lost enlightenment.
December 8th KATZ! explodes "got" and "lost."
In the snow, plum flowers one-by-one are red.

1. *"The Buddha saw a star, got enlightenment. Man Gong saw a star, lost enlightenment" – are they the same or different?*
2. *"December 8th KATZ! explodes 'got' and 'lost.' " What does this mean?*
3. *"In the snow, plum flowers one-by-one are red." What does this mean?*

COMMENTARY: Many stars in the sky. If you attain the Buddha's star, you will attain, "In the snow, plum flowers one-by-one are red."

160. Poem for Kan Wol Do Island

by Zen Master Man Gong

The man who is not close to the Buddha and
    eminent teachers –
Why does he make good friends with the blue
    ocean?
He is an original natural man,
So he stays in the natural.

1. *Why is the man not close to the Buddha and eminent teachers?*
2. *Who is he?*
3. *"He is an original natural man." What does this mean?*

COMMENTARY: Originally there is nothing. The Buddha and the original natural man come from where? If you want to understand the meaning of this, look at the palm of your hand.

161. Poem for Buddha's Birthday

by Zen Master Man Gong

Very tired, so the dream is very complicated:
This morning a bird gave a Dharma speech to
    me.
Today is Tiger Year's Buddha's Birthday.
One hundred grasses understand themselves:
    yellow and red.

1. *"This morning a bird gave a Dharma speech to me." What does this mean?*
2. *How do "One hundred grasses understand themselves: yellow and red"?*
3. *Originally nothing — so how does Buddha's birthday appear?*

COMMENTARY: Put it all down. What do you see now? What do you hear now?

162. Vairocana Peak*

Poem by Zen Master Man Gong

Autumn, 1925.
Man climbing up the blue sky.
The top of Vairocana is very bright –
A seal on the Eastern Ocean

---

*Highest Peak.

1. *How do you climb up the blue sky?*
2. *"The top of Vairocana is very bright." What does this mean?*
3. *If you have no Eastern Ocean, where is the seal?*

COMMENTARY: South Mountain is the body, North Ocean is the face. Walking in the sky, playing with the stars.

163. Poem for Tae Hwa Sahn Mountain

by Zen Master Man Gong

On the bones of the Great Mountain,
flowing water cleans the ancient Buddha's
mind.
Do you understand the true meaning of this?
You must ask the pine tree.

1. *How is the ancient Buddha's mind cleaned?*
2. *"You must ask the pine tree." What did the pine tree say?*

COMMENTARY: The road is very old. The man walking on it is very young, holding the pine tree and laughing.

164. Another Poem for Tae Hwa Sahn Mountain

by Zen Master Man Gong

Cloud and mountain have no same or
different –
That is the nothingness natural tradition.
If you get the nothingness seal,
Then you understand why the mountain is
blue.

1. *"Cloud and mountain have no same or different." What does this mean?*
2. *Did you attain the nothingness seal?*
3. *Why is the mountain blue?*

COMMENTARY: Originally there is nothing. Where do the sky, the ground, the mountains, and the rivers come from? Open your mouth, everything appears.

165. Kyol Che Poem

by Zen Master Man Gong

When Kyol Che begins, the stone girl has a
   dream.
When Kyol Che ends, the wooden man sings a
   song.
Dream and song, put it all down.
Look at the moon, bright as dark ink.

1. *What is the meaning of the stone girl's dream?*
2. *"Dream and song, put it all down." How do you do this?*
3. *What is the meaning of "The moon, bright as dark ink"?*

COMMENTARY: The mud cow flies to the moon. The moon says, "Ah, my stomach is very happy!"

166. Poem for a Student, Bo Wol

by Zen Master Man Gong

Form is emptiness; emptiness is also emptiness.
Form and emptiness – throw them both away.
Then what is this?
In wintertime, much ice.

1. *"Form and emptiness – throw them both away." Then what?*
2. *"In wintertime, much ice." What does this mean?*

COMMENTARY: Before you were born, you had no eyes, no ears, and no mouth. What do you call this? Understand that and hear universal sound.

167. Poem for Zen Master Un An*

by Zen Master Man Gong

Cloud appears, but never appears.
When it disappears, it also never disappears.
The place of never-appearing and never-
   disappearing;
Cloud rocks: spring without time.

1. *Where is the place of never-appearing and never-disappearing?*
2. *"Cloud rocks: spring without time." What does this mean?*

COMMENTARY: Open your mouth and everything appears; close your mouth and everything disappears. If you have no mouth, you are already complete.

168. Poem for a Bamboo Fan

by Zen Master Man Gong

The paper is not paper, the bamboo is not
   bamboo.
Clear wind comes from where?
The place without paper and bamboo.
Clear wind itself coming and going.

---

*Un An means "cloud rocks."

1. *"The place without paper and bamboo." What does this mean?*
2. *How does clear wind come and go?*

COMMENTARY: Is the wind from the fan or the paper? Don't check – only moving. Ah, wonderful!

| 169. *Prajna Ship*

Poem by Zen Master Man Gong

Everything is impermanent, but there is truth.
You and I are not two, not one:
Only your stupid thinking is nonstop.
Already alive in the Prajna ship.

1. *"Everything is impermanent, but there is truth." What does this mean?*
2. *"You and I are not two, not one." What does this mean?*
3. *"Already alive in the Prajna ship." What does this mean?*

COMMENTARY: What do you see now, what do you hear now? Everything appears clearly in front of you.

| 170. *Three Thousand KATZ's*

Poem by Zen Master Man Gong

Stepping to, stepping fro, what is this?
Falling down in the field, that is Vairocana
    Buddha.
Sometimes spit out, sometimes swallow heaven
    and earth.
Standing on Dok Sahn Mountain, three
    thousand KATZ's.

1. *What is stepping to and stepping fro?*
2. *How do you spit out and swallow heaven and earth?*

3. *What is the meaning of three thousand KATZ's?*

COMMENTARY: No eyes, no ears, no nose, no tongue, no body, no mind. But everything is standing right in front of you.

171. *Bo Dok Cave*

Poem by Zen Master Man Gong

Holding a bamboo stick, never stop.
Already arrive in front of Bo Dok cave.
Who is host, who is guest? They cannot see
    each other.
Only very close by, the gurgle of the stream.

1. *Why can't host and guest see each other?*
2. *How do you get close to the gurgle of the stream?*

COMMENTARY: The sound of the stream takes away both guest and host.

172. *Four Seasons*

Poem by Zen Master Seung Sahn

Flowers in the spring,
In the summer, cool breezes.
Leaves in the fall,
In winter, pure snow.

Is the world throwing me away?
Am I throwing away the world?
I lie in the Dharma room.
I don't care about anything.

White clouds floating in the sky,
Clear water flowing down the mountain,
The wind through the pagoda:
I surrender my whole life to them.

1. *Who made the four seasons?*
2. *This world and you, are they the same or different?*
3. *How do you surrender your whole life to the clouds, water and wind?*

COMMENTARY: The turning earth revolves around the sun, making the four seasons. If there were no sun, the four seasons would never appear. If you have no mind, you have no earth or sun. Are there four seasons then? Put it down, put it down! If you have nothing, lie down, only sleep.

173. *Enlightenment Day Poem*

by Zen Master Man Gong

In the sky, many stars.
Which star did the Buddha see?
Facing south, find the North Star.
That is the Buddha's enlightenment star.

1. *Which is the Buddha's enlightenment star?*
2. *How can you find the North Star while facing south?*
3. *How big is the Buddha's enlightenment star?*

COMMENTARY: Big mistake, big mistake. Put enlightenment down.

174. *Transmission Poem for Ko Bong**

by Zen Master Man Gong

The ancient Buddha never gave transmission.
How can I give transmission to you?
The cloud disappears, the moon by itself is
    bright.
Seung Sahn is Ko Bong.

1. *"The Ancient Buddha never gave transmission." What does this mean?*
2. *"The cloud disappears, the moon by itself is bright." Then what?*
3. *Seung Sahn and Ko Bong — are they the same or different?*

COMMENTARY: Form is emptiness, emptiness is form. Is the moonlight form or emptiness? Its face is very bright and beautiful.

175. *Zen Master Seung Sahn's Enlightenment Poem*

When Zen Master Seung Sahn was a young man, he went to Won Gak Sahn Mountain and did a one hundred-day solo retreat. During this retreat, he chanted the Great Dharani of Original Mind Energy continuously for twenty hours every day, and lived on a diet of crushed pine needles. After one hundred days, Seung Sahn attained enlightenment and composed the following poem:

---

*Ko Bong means "old peak." Seung Sahn is the name of the high mountain in China where the Seventh Patriarch lived and practiced.

The road at the bottom of Won Gak Sahn Mountain
is not the present road.
The man climbing with his backpack
is not a man of the past.
Tok, tok – his footsteps
transfix past and present.
Crows out of a tree.
Caw, caw, caw.

Soon afterward, Zen Master Seung Sahn was given formal Dharma Transmission by Zen Master Ko Bong.

1. *At the moment of his enlightenment, what did Zen Master Seung Sahn attain?*
2. *"Tok, tok – his footsteps transfix past and present." What does this mean?*
3. *"Crows out of a tree – Caw, caw, caw." What does this mean?*
4. *What did Seung Sahn get from Zen Master Ko Bong?*

COMMENTARY: Holy people understand holy people. Crazy people understand each other. What do you understand? It's already clear in front of you.

176. Zen Master Seung Sahn's Poem for Children

Children's Buddhist Sunday School
Hwa Gye Sah Temple, Seoul, 1981

Your mind is Buddha
My mind is also Buddha.
Buddha looks at Buddha,
Mind disappears.

Pine tree shadow reflected on the pond
is never wet.
Pebble thrown into the water,
Pine tree is dancing.

1. *Mind and Buddha, are they the same or different?*
2. *"Mind disappears." Where did it go?*
3. *"Pine tree is dancing." What does this mean?*

COMMENTARY: Clear mind, clear Buddha. No mind, no Buddha. But no mind is true Buddha. Which one is correct? Opening your mouth is already a big mistake. Children throw rocks into the pond. The pine tree is dancing.

177. Original Face

Poem by Zen Master Seung Sahn

Your true self is always
shining and free.

Human beings make something
and enter the ocean of suffering.

Only without thinking
can you return to your true self.
The high mountain is always blue.
White clouds coming, going.

1. *"Your true self is always shining." What does this mean?*
2. *How can you return to your true self?*
3. *Why are the clouds white and the mountain blue?*

COMMENTARY: Follow speech, lose your life. Follow meaning, go to hell. Open your eyes – what do you see now? What do you hear now? Original face and truth already appear in front of you.

178. Hae Jae Poem, Shin Won Sah Temple, 1989

by Zen Master Seung Sahn

Blue mountain, water flowing
For one thousand years.
Stone peak's whiteness
For numberless kalpas.

If you attain original Hae Jae,
Ten thousand mountains and valleys,
Only blue.

1. *When did color and time appear?*
2. *What is original Hae Jae?*
3. *When did mountains and valleys separate?*

COMMENTARY: The sky is my father, and ground is my mother. Mountain and water are my brother and sister. Clouds coming and going are my friends. My parents, my family, and my friends all have the same root. If you attain this root, everything is yours.

179. No Distinction

Poem by Zen Master Seung Sahn

Eyes seeing, but not seeing,
So no distinction.
Ears hearing, but no sound,
so no good or bad.

No distinction, no good or bad.
Everything – put it all down.
The blue mountain is complete stillness.
Moonlight shining everywhere.

1. *What does "no distinction" mean?*
2. *No good or bad, then what?*
3. *"Everything – put it all down." Why?*
4. *"The blue mountain is complete stillness." How does the moonlight shine everywhere?*

COMMENTARY: Eyes, ears, color, and sound are originally nothing. When did they appear? If you find that "when," you can attain your original face. If you cannot attain your original face, ask the stone girl. Rain falling down, the stone girl's dress is wet.

180. Enlightenment Poem

by Zen Master Hahn Am

Making rice over the fire, a great awakening.
The Lord of ancient Buddhas appears very
    clearly.
If somebody asks me why Bodhidharma came
    to China,
Under the rocks, flowing water-sound is never
    wet.

1. *What did Zen Master Hahn Am attain?*
2. *What is the meaning of "flowing-water sound is never wet?"*

COMMENTARY: The blue mountain is always blue. The big rocks never move.

181. North Mountain, South Mountain

Poem by Zen Master Hahn Am

Underfoot there is sky, overhead there is ground.
Originally there is no inside, no outside, no middle.
A person without legs is walking. A person without eyes sees something.
North Mountain keeps silence, facing South Mountain.

1. *What is the meaning of lines one, two and three?*
2. *"North Mountain keeps silence, facing South Mountain." Then what?*

COMMENTARY: Ask the North Mountain and the South Mountain. They will give you a good answer.

182. Mind Moonlight

Poem by Zen Master Hahn Am

Hear the dog barking and understand: guest coming.
The crow's caw disconcerts people.
Mind moonlight never changes for ten thousand years.
One morning the wind comes and cleans our yard.

What is the meaning of:

1. *"Hear the dog barking and understand: guest coming."*
2. *"Mind moonlight never changes for ten thousand years."*
3. *"One morning the wind comes and cleans our yard."*

COMMENTARY: If you see clearly and hear clearly, then everything appears clearly. But one thing has never appeared in front of you.

183. The Ten Thousand Samadhis Are Not Necessary

Poem by Zen Master Hahn Am

Deep pine tree valley:
Sitting quietly,
The moon was bright last night.
The ten thousand samadhis are not necessary.
When thirsty, drink.
When tired, sleep.

1. Why aren't the ten thousand samadhis necessary?
2. "When thirsty, drink. When tired, sleep." Why is meditation necessary?

COMMENTARY: Rockheads understand rockheads. Clever heads understand each other.

184. Peach Flowers Turn Pink

Poem by Zen Master Yong Song

The Buddha and eminent teachers originally
    don't understand.
I also don't understand.
Only spring comes and peach flowers turn
    pink.
Clear wind is blowing from the mountain.

1. *If the Buddha and eminent teachers don't understand, and if Zen Master Yong Song doesn't understand, how can he say that spring comes and peach flowers turn pink?*
2. *"Clear wind is blowing from the mountain." Then what?*

COMMENTARY: Silence is better than speech. Peach flowers teach you everything.

185. Zen Master So Sahn's Enlightenment Poem

Sitting quietly, only go straight for ten years.
Deep in the mountains, the birds are never
  afraid.
Last night, hard rain in the pine trees near the
  pond.
Horn appears on a fish head,
The crane cries three times.

1. *What did Zen Master So Sahn attain?*
2. *"Horn appears on a fish head, the crane cries three times." What does this mean?*

COMMENTARY: Use turtle hair to make a sweater. When the freezing wind blows, you will never be cold.

186. Moon and Wind

Poem by Zen Master So Sahn

River wind is flowing for 10,000 days.
Mountain moon is shining for 10,000 nights.
10,000 days and 10,000 nights of guests.
How many times standing on the porch with
  wind and moon?

1. What is "10,000 days and 10,000 nights of guests"?
2. How many times have you stood on the porch with wind and moon?

COMMENTARY: Facing the moon, the dog barks, "Woof, woof."

187. No White, No Blue

Poem by Zen Master Hyo Bong

Every day, human beings get older.
Every year, the mountain is blue.
Forget both human beings and the mountain –
Then there's no white, no blue.

1. How do you forget both human beings and the mountain?
2. No white, no blue. Then what?

COMMENTARY: When you open your mouth, everything appears and disappears. When you close your mouth, nothing appears or disappears. But if you have no mouth, you become Buddha.

188. The Ship with No Bottom

Poem by Zen Master Hyo Bong

If you want to take away the I-my-me
   mountain,
You must get a cane made of rabbit horn.
If you want to cross the ocean of suffering,
You must take the ship with no bottom.

1. Where do you get a cane made of rabbit horn?
2. Where is the ship with no bottom?

COMMENTARY: Opening your mouth cannot save you from hell. Close your mouth and you lose your life.

189. Plum Flowers Fly in the Snow

Dharma Master Hahn Yong Un recited his enlightenment poem to Zen Master Man Gong:

How many people stay in a worrying dream?
The great one's original home is everywhere.
One KATZ! sound breaks the whole world.
Plum flowers fly in the snow.

Man Gong replied, "Plum flowers fly in the snow. Where do they come down?"

"Turtle hair and rabbit's horn."

Man Gong laughed loudly, "Ha, ha, ha!" and asked the assembly, "What does that mean?"

One great nun, Poep Hi Sunim, came forward and said, "Snow melts, then ground appears."

"You've attained ground," Man Gong replied.

1. Where is a great one's original home?
2. "Plum flowers fly in the snow." What does that mean?
3. Man Gong asked where the plum flowers come down. How would you answer?
4. What is turtle hair and rabbit's horn?
5. "You've attained ground." What does that mean?

COMMENTARY: Wake up, wake up! Snow is white, the ground is brown.

190. Old Monk's Stick

Zen Master In Gak wrote a poem:

A long time ago, the Buddha stayed at Yong
    Sahn Mountain and picked a flower.
Only Mahakashyapa smiled.

One Zen Master commented: "This morning this old monk picks up a Zen stick. All gods and demons in the whole world are laughing!"

1. *Are the Buddha's flower and Mahakashyapa's smile the same or different?*
2. *Why, when the old monk picked up his Zen stick, did all the gods and demons laugh?*

COMMENTARY: Be careful, be careful! Look at something and you lose your heart.

191. *Good Time*

Poem by Zen Master Kyong Bong

Mountain is quiet,
Water is flowing,
Moon is bright,
Flower is blooming.
At midnight, a good smell fills the world.
A good time to drink tea.

1. *What do you attain from this poem?*
2. *What is a good time?*

COMMENTARY: Children like candy; the old man likes noodles.

192. *This World Is Complicated*

Poem by Zen Master Kyong Bong

Cold wind, eyes like jewels;
In the snow, a strong scent of plum flowers.
Many problems in this world, so it is very
        complicated.

But if you truly understand what this means,
Then you understand the correct way.

1. *Everything is complete. Why are there so many problems in this world and why is everything so complicated?*
2. *If you truly understand the meaning of the first two lines, then how do you understand the correct way?*

COMMENTARY: With no eyes, no ears, no nose, no tongue, and no body, everything appears clearly.

193. *Laughing Sounds*

Poem by Zen Master Jun Kang

Zen Master Jun Kang recited a poem to the assembly:

When you truly see this world, everything is
      just like this.
If your eyes are like Bodhidharma's,
Then there is much laughing and dancing!
The moon is bright in the sky;
The sun and stars are very quiet —
Only sounds of laughing fill the valley.

Then he commented, "Everybody heard these laughing sounds and got enlightenment."

1. *What are eyes like Bodhidharma's?*
2. *Why, if you have eyes like Bodhidharma's, is there laughing and dancing?*
3. *Did you hear the laughing sounds fill the valley?*

COMMENTARY: A great thief! Watch your pockets!!

194. The Clear, Mystic Thing

Zen Master Man Gong sat on a high stand to give a Dharma speech, declaring, "Originally the six roots, six dusts, and six consciousness are empty, but one clear mystic thing made everything. Did you find it? Where is it?" The whole assembly was silent. "Nobody understands, so I will show you one clear mystic thing. The mystic bird cannot dream on the tree. The mystic flower opens on the tree without shadow or roots."

1. Originally there are no six roots, six dusts, or six consciousnesses. Then what?
2. What is the meaning of the mystic bird?
3. What is the meaning of the mystic flower?

COMMENTARY: The bear catches the bird and laughs, "Ha, ha, ha!"

195. Attaining Don't-Know Is Your True Nature

One day Zen Master Ko Bong, seated on a high rostrum, hit his Zen stick on the table three times and composed this poem aloud:

If you want to understand,
You don't understand.
If you attain don't-know,
That is your true nature.

Then he said, "The Buddha sat under the Bodhi tree for six years, only don't-know. Bodhidharma sat in Sorim for nine years, also don't-know. If you want to understand something, you will go to hell like an arrow. If you attain don't-know you will get the Buddha's head and Bodhidharma's body. Even if you have a lot of money, a high position, many academic degrees, and great power, none of them can help your true self. If you take a rotten rope and tie it to a cloud, that will help your life a little bit. If you can put the whole world into a mustard seed, then you can understand your true nature. But at that time, what do you see, what do you hear? If you see or hear something you will go to hell. And if you cannot see or hear something you will lose your body. What can you do?"

Then holding up the Zen stick, he hit the table and said:

North mountain, white hair.
South stream, water flowing - DOL, DOL, DOL.

1. "If you attain don't-know you, that is your true nature." What does that mean?
2. The Buddha sat under the Bodhi tree for six years. Bodhidharma sat in Sorim for nine years. What did they get?
3. If you see or hear something you will go to hell. And if you cannot hear something you will lose your body. What can you do?
4. "North mountain, white hair. South stream, water flowing – DOL, DOL, DOL." What does that mean?

COMMENTARY: Watch out! Big thief!!

196. 25 O'clock

Sitting on the high rostrum, Zen Master Ko Bong hit his Zen stick three times and said, "The Buddha and all the eminent teachers don't understand this point and cannot give transmission of this point. If you go one step forward, you die; if you go one step backward, you die. Also, you cannot stay at this point. Nobody can help you. You can neither open your mouth nor move your body.

"How do you stay alive? If you stay alive, you are the same as the Buddha and all the eminent teachers, but you lose one leg and one eye. So where do you find one leg and one eye? Only go straight don't-know. If you pass 25 o'clock, you can find one leg and one eye. So how do you pass 25 o'clock?"

He held up the Zen stick, then hit the table three times and said, "Be careful! Be careful!!"

1. *Zen Master Ko Bong hit the table three times. Why can't the Buddha and all the eminent teachers attain this point?*
2. *You cannot do anything. How do you stay alive?*
3. *How do you pass 25 o'clock?*
4. *"Be careful! Be careful!!" What does this mean?*

COMMENTARY: Swallowed the ten directions, but still hungry.

197. "KAN!"

Zen Master Ko Bong, sitting on a high rostrum, hit his Zen Stick three times and said, "All great Zen Masters teach the whole world about one point. But this one point cannot be seen or heard, and it has no name and no form, so opening their mouths is already a big mistake. How can you make these great Zen Masters' teaching correct? If you want to do that, don't check good and bad, don't hold life and death, and put down your opinion and condition. Only go straight through the raging fires and attain no form, no emptiness. Then you will wake up to the wooden chicken's crowing."

Holding up his stick, he asked, "Do you see?" Then, hitting it on the table, "Do you hear?" He paused for a second, and then asked, "Did you find your original face? How many eyes are there?"

After a moment of silence he shouted, "KATZ!"

Then he said, "KAN!" ("Look!")

1. *All Zen Masters teach one point, but that one point is nothing. How do you teach nothing?*
2. *How do you get through the raging fire?*
3. *Did you hear the wooden chicken crowing?*
4. *What does "KAN!" mean?*

COMMENTARY: Open your mouth, you go to hell like an arrow. Close your mouth, you lose your life. What do you see now, what do you hear now? Just do it.

198. "MYUNG! MYUNG!"

One day Zen Master Ko Bong said from the high rostrum, "If you have no Dharma, you have no demon, but you fall into emptiness. If you are attached to emptiness, even the Buddha and Bodhidharma cannot save you. So it is important to make your Dharma very strong.

"How can you kill your demon? If you are a strong student your weapons are Great Faith, Great Courage and Great Question. But where do Great Faith, Great Courage and Great Question come from?

"If you make something, you cannot use these three weapons. If you don't make anything, you still cannot use them. What can you do? If you open your mouth, you go to hell. If you close your mouth, you are a rockhead. Do you understand that? I am giving you good medicine which will make all your sicknesses disappear. Then everything is complete."

Holding up his Zen stick and hitting the table, he said, "MYUNG! MYUNG!" ("Clear!")

1. *Dharma and demon, which one do you like?*
2. *How do you kill your demon?*
3. *How do you find Great Faith, Great Courage and Great Question?*
4. *"MYUNG! MYUNG!" What does it mean?*

COMMENTARY: The Buddha sat under the Bodhi tree for six years. Bodhidharma sat in Sorim for nine years. If you attain the true meaning of this, be careful about opening your mouth.

199. Zen Master Hahn Am's KATZ and Hit

Zen Master Hahn Am sat on the high rostrum in silence. He held up the Zen stick and hit the rostrum three times, and then shouted "KATZ!" three times. "If you find the Buddha's and eminent teachers' corpses in 'KATZ' and Hit, your original face already appears clearly," he said to the assembly. "If you cannot, you go to hell like an arrow."

1. *Silence, Hit, KATZ: are they the same or different?*
2. *Can you find your original face in KATZ or Hit?*
3. *What is the meaning of "Go to hell like an arrow"?*

COMMENTARY: Hahn Am never got out of hell. The Zen stick has already saved all beings.

200. Cloud Appears Over South Mountain

Zen Master Kyong Ho asked Zen Master Hahn Am, "Somebody hears 'Cloud appears over South Mountain, rain over North Mountain' and gets enlightenment. What do they attain?"

Zen Master Hahn Am replied, "In front of the meditation room there are many roof tiles."

1. *"Cloud appears over South Mountain, rain over North Mountain." What does that mean?*
2. *Is Zen Master Hahn Am's answer correct or not?*

COMMENTARY: If you see something, you become blind. If you hear something, you become deaf. If you open your mouth, you become mute. Without making anything, you already find a good answer.

201. You Don't Know. How Can I Teach You?

During the Japanese occupation of Korea, a Japanese Soto Zen Master visited Zen Master Hahn Am and asked, "What is Buddhism's true meaning?"

Hahn Am held up his glasses. Then the Japanese Zen Master said, "You are a great Zen Master. You have studied many sutras and meditated for many years. What did you attain?"

Hahn Am said, "You must go to the Palace of Silence and Stillness and bow."

Then the Japanese Zen Master asked, "You came to this temple in your youth and became a monk. You have stayed here for forty years. Your mind before coming here and your mind now – are they the same or different?"

Hahn Am replied, "You don't know. How can I teach you?"

1. *What is Buddhism's true meaning?*
2. *If you were Zen Master Hahn Am, what could you say you attained?*
3. *What is the meaning of "You don't know. How can I teach you"?*

COMMENTARY: Two bears wrestling, hit the rocks, fall down.

202. Hyo Bong's Enlightenment

Before Hyo Bong Sunim became a monk and ultimately a great Zen Master, he was a judge during the Japanese occupation of Korea. One day, the police brought a member of the Korean resistance movement before him. According to laws imposed by the Japanese, anyone convicted of resistance activities would be put to death. "What shall I do?" Hyo Bong thought. "If I act correctly as a judge, this man must die, but if I love my country, I cannot punish him." He became very confused, and could not do anything, so he resigned his position and devoted himself to studying the Buddha's teachings. After meeting Zen Master Im Sok Du at Shin Gae Sah Temple on Diamond Mountain, he shaved his head and became a monk.

Hyo Bong practiced very hard, sitting in meditation for hours with unmoving determination. He would never even lie down to sleep. One day a strong wind blowing through the pine trees caused a branch to snap. "Crack!" Upon hearing this sound, Hyo Bong got enlightenment, and composed the following poem:

> Under the sea is a dove's house. The dove is
> holding a deer's egg.
> In the fire-spider's house they're making fish
> tea.
> Who understands the family tradition?
> White cloud flies west, the moon running east.

1. *What is the meaning of the first and second lines?*
2. *What is the meaning of "White cloud flies west, the moon running east"?*

COMMENTARY: Wonderful, wonderful! A great man catches a cloud, turns it into a horse and flies into the sky.

203. A Gate

Zen Master Hyo Bong gave a Dharma speech in which he said: "There is a gate. From the East, this gate looks like the West Gate. From the West, this gate looks like the East Gate. From the South, it looks like the North Gate, and from the North, it looks like the South Gate. The three worlds of Buddhas, Bodhisattvas, and eminent teachers are all coming and going through this gate. How do you go through this gate?"

Holding his stick for a moment in silence, he hit the table and said, "If you come through this gate, I will hit you. If you go through this gate, I will also hit you. What can you do?"

1. *What is this gate?*
2. *Going or coming, Zen Master Hyo Bong will hit you. How do you pass this gate?*

COMMENTARY: Don't make anything, don't make anything. If you open your mouth, you have already passed through the gate to hell.

204. *Bodhidharma's Family Tradition*

During a Dharma speech, Zen Master Hyo Bong posed a kong-an to the assembly: "Three men are walking. The first man says, 'I am coming here just like this.' The second man says, 'I never come just like this.' The third man says, 'Put it all down.'

"Which one is correct? If you find this, I will hit you thirty times. If you cannot find this, I will also hit you thirty times. What can you do?" Nobody could answer. Then he made a poem:

> Write "Mu" in the sky –
> There is substance and great function.
> Meditation and enlightenment are important.
> But you must find Bodhidharma's family
>   tradition.

He then hit the table three times with his Zen stick and descended from the high stand.

1. *Of the three men, which one is correct?*
2. *How do you write "Mu" in the sky?*
3. *What are "substance and great function"?*
4. *What is Bodhidharma's family tradition?*

COMMENTARY: In the sky, one sun, one moon and many stars. But the blind man cannot see the sun, the moon or the stars.

主中主 | 205. Where Is the True Master?

Zen Master Hyo Bong once said to a group of students: "Front and back, right and left, everywhere is the true master. If you look for the true master, you will never find it, and you will never get out of the ocean of suffering. But I have a ship with no bottom. Everybody board this ship, and then you can get out of this ocean. All aboard! Hurry up, hurry up!"

Hitting the table with his Zen stick, Hyo Bong recited this poem:

> One step, two steps, three steps.
> Don't check around – only go straight.
> When water and mountain disappear,
> Your original home already appears.

1. *Your true master is everywhere. Do you see? Do you hear?*
2. *How do you ride the ship with no bottom?*
3. *What is the meaning of "When water and mountains disappear, your original home already appears"?*

COMMENTARY: Wake up from your dream! What do you see now? What do you hear now? The mountain is blue, the water is flowing.

206. Deceiving All Buddhas and Eminent Teachers

One day, Zen Master Hyo Bong delivered a Dharma speech from the high rostrum. "If you open your mouth, you deceive all Buddhas and eminent teachers. If you don't open your mouth, you deceive the whole assembly. How do you not deceive all Buddhas, eminent teachers and the assembly?"

Zen Master In Gak stood up and called out, "Attendant! One cup of tea for the Zen Master."

Then Hyo Bong said, "That's OK, but why didn't you pull me from the high stand? Today's Dharma speech is already finished, but somebody doesn't have enough mind, so I will make a poem for him:

> I look at this world.
> Nobody escapes life and death.
> If you want to take away your suffering,
> Throw life, death and Nirvana into the
> garbage."

1. *How do you not deceive all Buddhas, eminent teachers, and the assembly?*
2. *If at that time somebody appeared and pulled Zen Master Hyo Bong form the high stand, and if you were Hyo Bong, what could you do?*
3. *How do you throw life, death and Nirvana into the garbage?*

COMMENTARY: There are many stars in the sky, and many trees on the mountain. Birds sing in the trees. See clearly, hear clearly. Everything is complete. Silence is better than holiness.

207. Live Words and Dead Words

During a Dharma speech, Zen Master Hyo Bong said, "In our practice there are live words and dead words. If you attain live words, you are the same as the Buddha and eminent teachers. If you are attached to dead words, you never get out of the ocean of suffering. Live words and dead words are the same as dust in your eyes. So I ask you, how do you get the dust out of your eyes? Tell me! Tell me!" Hyo Bong was silent for a few moments, and then hit his Zen stick on the table three times and descended from the high stand.

1. *Live words and dead words: are they the same or different?*
2. *How do you get the dust out of your eyes?*
3. *Which are live words: silence or three hits of the Zen stick?*

COMMENTARY: Who can save Hyo Bong? If you want to save him, you must use a hammer with no handle.

208. *Appearing and Disappearing*

Zen Master Hyo Bong once said, "Everything is appearing and disappearing. But everything comes from complete stillness. This stillness is substance. If you attain substance, you attain truth and correct function. Then appearing and disappearing are truth, and the correct function of appearing and disappearing is possible.

"My question to all of you is, where do substance, truth and function come from? If you open your mouth, you already make opposites. If you close your mouth, you are attached to emptiness. How do you, with your mouth not open and not closed, attain substance, truth and function?"

Nobody could answer.

"I'll give you a hint," he continued. "KATZ! Everybody return to your rooms and drink tea."

1. *Are appearing, disappearing, and stillness the same or different?*
2. *What is substance? What is truth? What is function?*
3. *What is the meaning of "KATZ!" and "Return to your rooms and drink tea"?*

COMMENTARY: Aigo, aigo, aigo! Where do you find Hyo Bong's original body? Watch your step!

209. *Zen Master Hyo Bong's Three Gates*

First Gate: There is an animal on Maitreya Mountain which has the body of a dog and the head of a tiger. What do you call it? Is it a tiger or a dog?

Second Gate: There is a dark moon and a white moon in the sky. The dark moon is going from west to east. The white moon is going from east to west. The two moons come together and become one. What does this mean?

Third Gate: The whole world is a furnace. How did part of it get to be snow?

COMMENTARY: One action is better than ten thousand words.

210. *Ten Mu Sicknesses*

Zen Master Yong Song received a visit from Zen Master Ko Am, and asked his guest, "In Joju's Mu kong-an there are ten kinds of sickness. How do you not get sick?"

"I'm only walking on the edge of the sword," Ko Am replied.

1. *What are the ten Mu sicknesses?*
2. *"Walking on the edge of the sword." What does this mean?*

COMMENTARY: Go ask a cow. You will get a beautiful answer.

211. Lion's Den

Zen Master Yong Song asked Zen Master Ko Am, "What is the meaning of the Buddha's picking up a flower and showing it to Mahakashyapa?"

Zen Master Ko Am answered, "In the lion's den there are no other animals."

1. *What is the meaning of the Buddha's picking up a flower and showing it to Mahakashyapa?*
2. *Why are there no other animals in the lion's den?*

COMMENTARY: Mistake, mistake, mistake. If you attain the Buddha's mistake, you will attain the Buddha's flower.

212. The Sky Is High, the Ground Is Thick

Zen Master Yong Song once asked Zen Master Ko Am, "The Sixth Patriarch said, 'The flag is not moving, the wind is not moving. Your mind is moving.' What does this mean?"

Zen Master Ko Am stood up, bowed three times and answered, "The sky is high, the ground is thick."

1. *If you were Zen Master Ko Am, how would you answer?*
2. *What is the meaning of "The sky is high, the ground is thick"?*

COMMENTARY: Hear a sound, fall down. See something, lose your life.

213. *Dharma Transmission*

佛

祖

識不

得

Ko Am asked Zen Master Yong Song, "What is your family teaching tradition?"

Zen Master Yong Song, holding a Zen stick, hit the table three times and said, "What is your family teaching tradition?" Ko Am took the stick and hit the table three times. Then Yong Song said, "Moonlight for 10,000 years," and gave him *inga* and transmission. Then he wrote this poem for Ko Am:

Transmission Poem

The Buddha and eminent teachers originally
     don't know;
Shaking my head, I also don't know.
Un Mun's cake is round.
Chinju's *mu** is long.

1. *Are Zen Master Yong Song's tradition and Zen Master Ko Am's tradition the same or different?*
2. *What is the meaning of "Moonlight for 10,000 years"?*
3. *How big is Un Mun's cake?*
4. *How long is Chinju's mu?*

COMMENTARY: Yong Song and Ko Am hug each other and fall down into an old well.

214. *What Is One Thing?*

Zen Master Yong Song once gave a Dharma speech, in which he said, "Everyone has one thing. This one thing swallowed heaven, earth, and everything. If you want to find it, it's already far away. If you put it down, it's always in front of you. Brighter than the sun and darker than black ink, it always abides under your palm. Have you found it?"

---

*"Mu" means "radish."

1. *How did one thing swallow everything?*
2. *What is the meaning of "If you want to find it, it's far away. If you put it down, it's always in front of you"?*
3. *What is the meaning of "Brighter than the sun and darker than black ink"?*
4. *Have you found it under your palm?*

COMMENTARY: If the Sixth Patriarch were there, he would have hit Yong Song right in the face.

215. *Dong Sahn's Zen Stick*

Holding his Zen stick, Zen Master Dong Sahn said from the high rostrum, "If you say that this is a Zen stick, it will hit you thirty times. If you say that is not a Zen stick, it will also hit you thirty times. If you can find the original Zen stick's substance, you will go beyond life and death and attain the land of Buddha. How can you, without speech, attain this Zen stick's substance?"

Then, hitting the table with his stick, he said, "Hit the leg of Blue Mountain, then pick up the East Ocean's head."

1. *How do you attain the Zen stick's substance?*
2. *How do you attain the land of Buddha?*
3. *"Hit the leg of Blue Mountain, then pick up the East Ocean's head." What does that mean?*

COMMENTARY: Correct action is better than the Buddha's speech.

216. *Dragon Tracks*

Zen Master Dong Sahn, sitting on the high rostrum, hit his Zen stick three times and said, "Human beings are coming and going on a bridge. This bridge is flowing, while the water underneath is not flowing. An eminent teacher once said, 'when there is no dream, no thinking, and no action, where is your true master?'"

After a moment of silence he continued, "Everybody at this moment has attained their true self. Coming and going, you are completely free. But there is still a single hair on your head. How can you take away that single hair?"

Holding up the Zen stick, then hitting the table, he said, "Sitting, cut off all thinking and look in the ten directions. There you will see dragon tracks."

1. *"Human beings are coming and going on a bridge. This bridge is flowing while the water underneath is not flowing." What does this mean?*
2. *No dream, no thinking, no action. Where is your true master?*
3. *How do you take away one single hair?*
4. *How do you find dragon tracks in the ten directions?*

COMMENTARY: Open your mouth, lose your tongue. Close your mouth, lose your life. What are you doing just now? Just do it!

217. *"GAM" and "EEE"*

Zen Master Dong Sahn, hitting the table with his Zen stick, said, "Leaves from a maple tree fell down a deep well, and heaven and earth appeared. A long time ago Zen Master Un Mun, sitting on a high rostrum, looked at the assembly, and shouted, 'GAM!' ("gam" means look.) A monk stood up to ask a question of Un Mun, but right at that moment the Zen Master shouted, 'EEE!' ("eee" means sad.) If you attain those two sounds, 'GAM!' and 'EEE!,' you attain live Zen. If you don't understand those two words, you only have dead Zen."

Then Dong Sahn said, "What are Un Mun's 'GAM' and 'EEE?' Are they the same or different?"

Everybody was silent, so Dong Sahn composed a poem:

Looking at each other, not moving an eyelash:
You are east, I am west.
Western dawn across the ocean,
Bright sun through Sumi Mountain.

1. *Where are the leaves of the maple tree?*
2. *What do the Zen Master's "GAM" and "EEE" mean?*
3. *What is live Zen and what is dead Zen?*
4. *How does the sun get through Sumi Mountain?*

COMMENTARY: Don't make anything. See and hear clearly.
The moon rises in the West, the sun sets in the West.

218. *The Stone Lion's Roar*

One of the most famous monks in all of
Thailand visited Zen Master Dong Sahn. The
great Korean Zen Master warmly received his
guest, saying, "When I went to your country,
you gave me many beautiful presents and did many kind
deeds for me, so today I would like to give you a present." He
then pointed to a stone lion and said, "Do you see this lion?"
"Yes."
"Do you hear the lion's roar?"
The monk was completely dumbfounded, and could not
answer.
Zen Master Dong Sahn said, "That is my present to you."

1. *Do you hear the stone lion's roar?*
2. *What was Zen Master Dong Sahn's present to the monk
from Thailand?*

COMMENTARY: Don't tell your dream to a rockhead.

219. Moon Guest

Once a monk asked Zen Master Gum Oh, "What is Buddha?"

"There is a bright moon in the sky and guests are coming."

1. *"There is a bright moon in the sky and guests are coming." What does that mean?*
2. *If you were the monk, what could you say to this?*

COMMENTARY: The Sixth Patriarch said, "Originally nothing." If you make something, you lose your life.

220. If You Want to Meet the Buddha

Zen Master Gum Oh told a group of his students, "Everybody understands where the Buddha's house is. It's called the Palace of Stillness and Extinction. The palace columns are made of rabbit's horn, and the roof of turtle's hair. If you find this palace and open the door, you will meet the true Buddha."

1. *Where is the Palace of Stillness and Extinction?*
2. *How do you make rabbit's horn columns and a turtle's hair roof?*
3. *How do you open the door of the palace and meet the true Buddha?*

COMMENTARY: If you have ears, you lose your life. If you have no ears, you are better than the Buddha.

221. *Dharma Without Eyes, Ears or Mouth*

Zen Master Gum Oh once said, "If you see something, you are blind. If you hear something, you are deaf. If you open your mouth, you are dumb. So how can you teach the Dharma to all beings?"

What is the meaning of:

1. *"If you see something, you are blind."*
2. *"If you hear something, you are deaf."*
3. *"If you open your mouth, you are dumb."*
4. *No eyes, no ears, no mouth: how do you help all beings?*

COMMENTARY: Look, look! Big thief! No mind, no problem. If you have mind, it is already stolen.

222. *Oriole and Stork*

Zen Master Jun Kang composed a poem aloud:

An oriole sitting in the tree
becomes a flower.
A stork standing in the garden
becomes a patch of snow.

Then he said, "That is Buddha's mind. But if you attain Buddha from the poem, you will lose your body. If you don't attain Buddha from this poem, this stick will hit you thirty times. What can you do?"

After a moment of silence he said, "Already appeared."

1. *Did you find Buddha in this poem?*
2. *"If you attain Buddha from this poem, you will lose your body." Why?*
3. *After a moment he said, "Already appeared." What does this mean?*

223. No Nostrils

Sitting on the high rostrum before a large assembly of monks, Zen Master Jun Kang hit his Zen stick three times and said, "When our grandteacher Kyong Ho got enlightenment he wrote a poem:

When I hear somebody say "no nostrils,"
I know three thousand worlds are my home.
Yong Nam Mountain in June –
A free man makes a peace song.

"The first and second lines are very good, but the last line has a mistake. If you find this mistake, you attain Zen Master Kyong Ho's mind. If you cannot find the mistake, you are a blind dog."

1. *What did Zen Master Kyong Ho attain?*
2. *Jun Kang said that the last line has a mistake. Where is it?*
3. *Zen Master Jun Kang said, "If you find the mistake, you attain Zen Master Kyong Ho's mind." What does this mean?*

COMMENTARY: The clever man sees a rope and makes a snake out of it. The stupid man sees a rock and bows.

224. Hanging On a Vine

Zen Master Yong Sahn sent this story to all the Zen Masters in Korea, and asked them to write back with a response:

"A man was being chased by a wild elephant across a field. He stumbled into an old well, and as he was falling, grabbed hold of a vine which was hanging from the inside of the well. He looked down and saw three poisonous snakes at the bottom of the well, while above, the elephant was still waiting for him. A black mouse and a white mouse began gnawing on the vine just as honey from a plant growing on the side of the well began dripping into his mouth. If you were this man, how could you stay alive?"

Each Zen Master sent a reply:

Man Gong: "Last night I had a dream, so I woke up."

Hae Wol: "If you want to understand, you cannot understand. Only don't-know."

Hae Bong: "Buddha cannot see Buddha."

Yong Sahn: "Flower falls down, flax in the garden."

Bo Wol: "How do you fall into the well?"

Jun Kang: "Sweet!"

Ko Bong and Hyong Gak both wrote, "Aigo, aigo!"

Chung Soeng: Only laughing.

Hae Am: "Already dead."

Tan Ho: "Water flowing, never stopping."

1   *If you were there at that time, how could you stay alive?*
2.   *Which one is the best answer?*

COMMENTARY: Be careful. Open your mouth, already a big mistake. Thinking, you lose your life. Just do it.

| 225. *Half a Mu*

One morning, Zen Master Jun Kang visited Zen Master Hae Bong at Mah Gok Sah Temple and said to him, "I don't like Joju's 'Mu.' I like half a 'Mu.' Please give me half a 'Mu.'"

Hae Bong said, "Mu!"

"That's not half a 'Mu.'"

"Then what is half a 'Mu?'"

Jun Kang said, "Mu!"

Laughing hard, Hae Bong said, "You are very clever."

1. *Joju said "Mu," and that is a big mistake. Where is Joju's mistake?*
2. *If somebody asks you to give half a "Mu," what can you say?*

COMMENTARY: Two mud cows, wrestling, fall into the ocean. Which one wins, which one loses? No news.

226. *Originally Nothing*

When Zen Master Jun Kang visited Zen Master Hae Am at the Diamond Mountain Ji Jang Bosal Temple, Hae Am asked him, "The Sixth Patriarch wrote 'Originally nothing,' and then got transmission. What did he get?" Jun Kang only clapped his hands three times.

1. *What does "Originally nothing" mean?*
2. *Is Jun Kang's answer correct or not?*

COMMENTARY: Mistake, mistake, mistake. A second offense is not permitted. You must ask the stone girl.

227. *First Word*

Zen Master Jun Kang visited Zen Master Yong Song and was asked, "What is the first word?"
"Yes!"
"No!" Yong Song replied.
Jun Kang clapped his hands and laughed.
Yong Song again said, "No!"
"I ask you, then, what is the first word?"
"Jun Kang!"
"Yes!" Jun Kang replied.
"That is the first word," Yong Song said.

1. *What is the first word?*
2. *What is the last word?*

COMMENTARY: If you open your mouth, the first word and last word both appear. If you close your mouth, they both disappear. Without any mouth, the first and last word are already clear.

228. Hair Grows on Wide Teeth

Zen Master Jun Kang always posed the following kong-an to his students: "A long time ago, someone asked Zen Master Joju, 'Why did Bodhidharma come to China?' Joju replied, 'Hair grows on wide teeth.' If you attain this you can see Bodhidharma's true face. If you don't understand this, you don't know Joju or Bodhidharma."

1. *"Hair grows on wide teeth." What does that mean?*
2. *What is Bodhidharma's true face?*
3. *"If you don't understand this, then you don't know Joju or Bodhidharma." What does this mean?*

COMMENTARY: The snake's beard grows for a thousand miles. The rabbit's horn grows and pierces the moon.

229. Thorny Jungle Everywhere

Zen Master Jun Kang gave a Dharma speech from the high rostrum, saying, "Upon his enlightenment, Zen Master Man Gong composed this poem:

Empty mountain, true energy without time and
space.
White cloud and clear wind come and go by
themselves.
Why did Bodhidharma come to China?
Rooster crowing in the morning,
Sun rising in the east.

Then Jun Kang said, "If you attain this poem, you attain the
meaning of all the sutras. The last two lines are the most
important: 'Rooster crowing in the morning, Sun rising in the
east.'"

"If you find that point, then you find Bodhidharma's heart
and the Buddha's head. So I ask you, where is Bodhidharma's
heart and Buddha's head?"

After holding up the Zen stick in silence for a moment, he
shouted, "KATZ!"

Then he said, "Thorny jungle everywhere."

1. *What did you attain from Zen Master Man Gong's poem?*
2. *Zen Master Jun Kang said, "If you find that point, you find
   Bodhidharma's heart and the Buddha's head." What does
   this mean?*
3. *"Thorny jungle everywhere." What does this mean?*
4. *How do you get out of this thorny jungle?*

COMMENTARY: Look, look! Big thief! Watch your pockets.

| 230. True Emptiness

Zen Master Jun Kang visited Zen Master Hae
Wol, and was asked, "What does true emptiness
and stillness mystic wisdom mean?"
Jun Kang replied, "Cannot hear, cannot see."
"No," Hae Wol said.
"Cannot hear, cannot see!"
But Hae Wol said, "Big mistake!"

1. *What is emptiness and stillness mystic wisdom?*
2. *Where is Jun Kang's mistake?*

COMMENTARY: Two stone girls face each other. Together they laugh, "Ha, ha, ha!"

231. Ma Jo's Circle

One day Zen Master Bo Wol asked Zen Master Jun Kang, "A long time ago, Zen Master Ma Jo said to the assembly, 'I have a circle. If you enter this circle I will hit you. If you do not enter this circle, I will also hit you. What can you do?' So I ask you, Jun Kang, if you had been there, how would you have answered?"

Jun Kang replied, "I don't like nonsense. How do you not get hit by Ma Jo's stick?"

Bo Wol answered, "Why are you holding Ma Jo's stick?"

1. *If you had been there, how would you have answered Ma Jo's question?*
2. *Where is Jun Kang's mistake?*

COMMENTARY: Your feet are walking on the ground. Your arms are moving back and forth.

232. Ko Bong's No Hindrance Person

Many years ago, the Chinese Zen Master Ko Bong said to a group of monks, "There is a person who is made of nothing but skin with holes, rotting flesh, and broken bones, but still this person's speech is no hindrance. How wonderful! This person's actions, coming and going, hit and break all space, and swallow the big ocean.

"If you want to know who this is, you must understand the following: The mud cow eats the steel stick and spits blood on the guardian angel."

1. *Nothing but skin with holes, rotting flesh, and broken bones. How do you become a person with no hindrance?*
2. *How does the person with no hindrance swallow the big ocean?*
3. *Where is the mud cow?*
4. *Who is the guardian angel?*

COMMENTARY: Blood fills the sky. Bone appears all over the earth. How can you breathe clean air? How do you walk around in the ten directions? Watch your step!

233. *Mistake*

Zen Master Kyong Bong, sitting before an assembly, hit his Zen stick on the rostrum and said, "All Buddhas and all eminent teachers made a big mistake, because opening one's mouth is already a mistake. So how do you correct all the Buddhas and eminent teachers? If you make their mistake correct, this stick will hit you thirty times. If you do not make their mistake correct, this stick will also hit you thirty times. What can you do?"

After holding the stick a moment in silence, he said:

> The geese with no shadows
> Fly in cold moonlight.
> Stone lion running east,
> North star moving west.

After another moment of silence he shouted, "KATZ!" then commented, "And this is also a big mistake."

1. *Where is all Buddhas' and eminent teachers' mistake?*
2. *What does the Zen Master's poem mean?*
3. *At the end he said, "And this is also a big mistake." What does this mean?*

COMMENTARY: This stick has already hit Zen Master Kyong Bong thirty times. Aigo, aigo, aigo!

234. Where Is Your Hometown?

One winter, Zen Master Chun Song stayed at Nang Wol Sah Temple. It was very cold, and there were many students there for Kyol Che, so the Zen Master told the students to cut down some trees for firewood. But there was a law against cutting down trees, so a policeman came and took Chun Song to the police station.

The policeman asked him, "Why did you cut down the trees?"

"Because it's cold and we have no wood."

"That is illegal! Where is your hometown?"

The Zen Master answered, "My father's X X X."

"WHAT!? Where is your hometown?"

The Zen Master said, "I already told you – my father's X X X."

The policeman yelled, "Are you crazy?"

"No," said the Zen Master.

"Where do you come from?" asked the policeman.

"From my mother's X X X."

"WHAT!?"

"I already said, from my mother's X X X."

"You're crazy!!" the policeman shouted. "Go away!" And so Zen Master Chun Song was released.

1. *Why did Chun Song cut down the trees?*
2. *Is this Zen Master crazy, or is he a Bodhisattva?*

COMMENTARY: The crying boy wants candy. The old woman likes donuts.

235. One Pure and Clear Thing

One day Zen Master Man Gong gave a Dharma speech in which he said, "Even if this world explodes, if everyone has one pure and clear

147

thing, it will never disappear. That thing sometimes dreams, sometimes is awake. Then I ask you, not-dreaming and not-awake, where is it?"

1. *When everything explodes, where is the one pure and clear thing?*
2. *During not-dreaming time and not-awake time, where does it stay?*

COMMENTARY: When you are hungry, go to the kitchen. When you are tired, go to the bedroom.

236. What Is Bodhi?

After sitting a few moments in silence on the high rostrum, Zen Master Man Gong hit the table with his stick and said, "Bodhi mind comes from here. Standing on one foot on the top of a high mountain. Don't ask North, South, East, West. Bodhidharma doesn't understand Bodhi. How do you understand Bodhi? Today I will show you true Bodhi: listen carefully, listen carefully!" He hit the table three times and descended from the high rostrum.

1. *What is Bodhi?*
2. *What is the meaning of "Standing on one foot on the top of a high mountain?"*
3. *Why doesn't Bodhidharma understand Bodhi?*
4. *The Zen Master hit the table three times. Is that Bodhi?*

COMMENTARY: Wonderful, wonderful. One-man show, without hands or legs.

237. No Mind, No Dharma

Zen Master Chun Song, sitting on the high rostrum, hit his Zen stick three times and said, "Even if you have Dharma, you must take away

Dharma. Why make new Dharma?

"Where does this Dharma come from? From your mind. When mind appears, everything appears. When mind disappears, everything disappears. So where do you find Dharma? And if you have no Dharma, you have no mind, so how can you save all beings?

"Lin Chi's 'KATZ!,' Dok Sahn's hit, Guji's one finger – are they Dharma or are they mind? If you say they are Dharma, you have already made hell. If you say they are mind, you are already dead. How do you, with no Dharma and no mind, save all beings?"

After a moment of silence he struck the table and said, "When the stone girl has a baby, you will understand."

1. *No Dharma, no mind. How do you save all beings?*
2. *Lin Chi's 'KATZ!,' Dok Sahn's hit, and Guji's one finger – are they Dharma or are they mind?*
3. *When the stone girl has a baby, what do you attain?*

COMMENTARY: How wonderful – a great man! Mind is straight, speech is straight.

238. *Name and Tao*

The Tao that can be told
is not the eternal Tao.
The name that can be named
is not the eternal name.
The unnameable is the eternally real.
Naming is the origin
of all particular things.

1. *"The Tao that can be told is not the eternal Tao." What does that mean?*
2. *What is not the eternal Tao?*
3. *"Naming is the origin of all particular things." What does that mean?*

COMMENTARY: Clouds in the sky, blue mountains. A woman is laughing, "Ha, ha, ha!"

239. Done and Undone

In the pursuit of knowledge,
every day something is added.
In the practice of the Tao,
every day something is dropped.
Less and less do you need to force things,
until finally you arrive at non-action.
When nothing is done,
nothing is left undone.

True mastery can be gained
by letting things go their own way.
It can't be gained by interfering.

1. *In practicing the Tao, how do you practice the Tao?*
2. *Who made "done" and "undone"?*
3. *How do you let things go their own way?*

COMMENTARY: Everything is complete and unmoving, never changing, but opening your mouth is already a big mistake. The tree, the rock, the dog, and the cat are better than you because they only *do* it.

240. Doing Anything

Therefore the Master
acts without doing anything
and teaches without saying anything.
Things arise and she lets them come;
things disappear and she lets them go.
She has but doesn't possess,
acts but doesn't expect.
When her work is done, she forgets it.
That is why it lasts forever.

1. *"Therefore the Master acts without doing anything." What does this mean?*
2. *"She has but doesn't possess, acts but doesn't expect." How can you do that?*

COMMENTARY: If you are holding something, you will go straight to hell like an arrow. If you are not holding anything, you will lose your body. Seeing clearly, hearing clearly, just do it.

241. Lose Everything

The Master leads
by emptying people's minds
and filling their cores,
by weakening their ambition
and toughening their resolve.
He helps people lose everything
they know, everything they desire,
and creates confusion in those
who think that they know.
Practice not-doing,
and everything will fall into place.

1. "The Master leads by emptying people's minds and filling their cores." What does that mean?
2. "He helps people lose everything." How does he help people lose everything?
3. "Practice not-doing, and everything will fall into place." How will everything fall into place?

COMMENTARY: If you open your mouth, everything appears. If you close your mouth, everything disappears. Before you were born, no mouth: never open, never closed. At that time, what is everything? The cow doesn't care about your mouth, only "Moo, moo!" The dog doesn't think about your mouth, and only barks, "Woof, woof!"

242. The Tao Is Like a Well

The Tao is like a well:
used but never used up.

It is like the eternal void:
filled with infinite possibilities.

It is hidden but always present.
I don't know who gave birth to it.
It is older than God.

1. *"The Tao is like a well: used but never used up." What does this mean?*
2. *"It is hidden but always present." That "present" – does it exist or not?*
3. *"[The Tao] is older than God." What does that mean?*

COMMENTARY: The river waters are always flowing, without stopping. The mountain never opens its mouth.

243. *Before Tao and Master*

The Tao doesn't take sides;
it gives birth to both good and evil.
The Master doesn't take sides;
she welcomes both saints and sinners.

The Tao is like a bellows:
it is empty yet infinitely capable.
The more you use it, the more it produces;
the more you talk of it, the less you understand.

Hold on to the center.

1. *Before Tao and before Master, what?*
2. *"The Tao is like a bellows: it is empty yet infinitely capable." How does it help human beings?*
3. *"Hold on to the center." How do you hold on to the center?*

COMMENTARY: Understand one, understand two. Without understanding one, you are complete.

244. The Great Mother

The Tao is called the Great Mother:
empty yet inexhaustible,
it gives birth to infinite worlds.

It is always present within you.
You can use it any way you want.

1. *"The Tao is called the Great Mother: empty yet inexhaustible, it gives birth to infinite worlds." How does it give birth to infinite worlds?*
2. *"It is always present within you." Are you and the Tao the same or different?*

COMMENTARY: The child calls out to its mother – it wants milk. The sky has no inside, no outside, only blue.

245. Present for All Beings

The Tao is infinite, eternal.
Why is it eternal?
It was never born;
thus it can never die.
Why is it infinite?
It has no desires for itself;
thus it is present for all beings.

The Master stays behind;
that is why she is ahead.
She is detached from all things;
that is why she is one with them.
Because she has let go of herself,
she is perfectly fulfilled.

1. *"The Tao is infinite, eternal. It has no desires for itself." What does that mean?*
2. *Tao, Master, and she – who is first?*

COMMENTARY: On the freeway, the cars never stop. The woman waves her hand to call her child.

246. The Tao Is Like Water

The supreme good is like water,
which nourishes all things without trying to.
It is content with the low places that people
     disdain.
Thus it is like the Tao.

1. *The Tao is like water. So, is dirty water also the Tao?*

COMMENTARY: Western people like coffee. Eastern people like green tea.

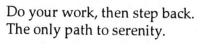

247. Path to Serenity

Do your work, then step back.
The only path to serenity.

1. *"Do your work, then step back." How do you do that?*
2. *For whom do you do that?*

COMMENTARY: The mouse likes cheese; the cat likes the mouse.

248. The Supreme Virtue

Giving birth and nourishing,
having without possessing,
acting with no expectations,
leading and not trying to control:
this is the supreme virtue.

1. *Giving, having, acting, leading. How do you keep that mind?*
2. *"This is the supreme virtue." What does that mean?*

COMMENTARY: Originally nothing. Condition appears and becomes red and white. But if you are not attached to red and white, you are free.

249. Open as the Sky

Colors blind the eye.
Sound deafens the ear.
Flavors numb the taste.
Thoughts weaken the mind.
Desires wither the heart.

The Master observes the world
but trusts his inner vision.
He allows things to come and go.
His heart is open as the sky.

1. *Blind, deaf, numb, weak. Then what's happening?*
2. *Are the Master and the world one or two?*
3. *"His heart is open as the sky." What does this mean?*

COMMENTARY: Dogs chase bones. The cicada in the tree sings, "Wing, wing, wing."

250. Love and World

See the world as your self.
Have faith in the way things are.
Love the world as your self;
then you can care for all things.

1. *The world and your self. Do they exist or are they emptiness?*
2. *What does it mean to love the world as your self?*
3. *How can you care for all things?*

COMMENTARY: South, north, east, west. The rising sun is bright everywhere.

251. The Essence of Wisdom

Look, and it can't be seen.
Listen, and it can't be heard.
Reach, and it can't be grasped.

Above, it isn't bright.
Below, it isn't dark.
Seamless, unnameable,
it returns to the realm of nothing.
Form that includes all forms,
image without an image,
subtle, beyond all conceptions.

Approach it and there is no beginning;
follow it and there is no end.
You can't know it, but you can be it,
at ease in your own life.
Just realize where you come from:
this is the essence of wisdom.

1. *"Follow it and there is no end." What does this mean?*
2. *"You can't know it, but you can be it." What is it?*
3. *What is "the essence of wisdom?"*

COMMENTARY: An old man carries his grandson on his back. The dog follows in front and back.

252. Where Is Serenity?

Empty your mind of all thoughts.
Let your heart be at peace.
Watch the turmoil of beings,
but contemplate their return.

Each separate being in the universe
returns to the common source.
Returning to the source is serenity.

1. *"Empty your mind of all thoughts." If your mind is empty, how do thoughts appear?*
2. *"Each separate being in the universe. . ." Who made the universe?*
3. *"Returning to the source is serenity." Where is serenity?*

COMMENTARY: The cars are driving on the freeway; the train is running on the tracks. The children wave their hands, "Hello, hello, hello!"

253. *His Work Is Done*

When the Master governs, the people
are hardly aware that he exists.
Next best is a leader who is loved.
Next, one who is feared.
The worst is one who is despised.

If you don't trust the people,
you make them untrustworthy.

The Master doesn't talk, he acts.
When his work is done,
the people say, "Amazing:
we did it, all by ourselves!"

1. *How does the Master govern the people?*
2. *"When his work is done," then what?*
3. *How did you do it all by yourself?*

COMMENTARY: The woman carries the baby and gives it milk. The man goes into the mountains and chops firewood.

254. *Forget the Tao*

When the great Tao is forgotten,
goodness and piety appear.
When the body's intelligence declines,
cleverness and knowledge step forth.
When there is no peace in the family,
filial piety begins.
When the country falls into chaos,
patriotism is born.

1. *How do you forget the Tao?*
2. *"Goodness and piety appear." How?*
3. *"When the country falls into chaos, patriotism is born." How do you become a patriot?*

COMMENTARY: The hero kills many enemies to help his country. Where will he repent?

255. *Throw It Away*

Throw away holiness and wisdom,
and people will be a hundred times happier.
Throw away morality and justice,
and people will do the right thing.
Throw away industry and profit,
and there won't be any thieves.

If these three aren't enough,
just stay at the center of the circle
and let all things take their course.

1. *How do you throw away those things?*
2. *What does it mean to "stay at the center of the circle?"*

COMMENTARY: Originally nothing – what do you throw away? Be careful: a second offense is not permitted.

256. This Is True

The Master keeps her mind
always at one with the Tao;
that is what give her her radiance.

The Tao is ungraspable.
How can her mind be at one with it?
Because she doesn't cling to ideas.

The Tao is dark and unfathomable.
How can it make her radiant?
Because she lets it.

Since before time and space were,
the Tao is.
It is beyond *is* and *is not*.
How do I know this is true?
I look inside myself and see.

1. *The Master, her mind, and the Tao — how do they become one?*
2. *"The Tao is ungraspable. How can her mind be at one with it?" What is it?*
3. *"How do I know this is true?"*

COMMENTARY: Everything is the Tao, and everything is not the Tao. Which one is correct? When you are thirsty, have a drink. When you are hungry, just eat.

257. Truly Yourself

The Master, by residing in the Tao,
sets an example for all beings.
Because he doesn't display himself,
people can see his light.
Because he has nothing to prove,
people can trust his words.
Because he doesn't know who he is,
people recognize themselves in him.

Because he has no goal in mind,
everything he does succeeds.

When the ancient Masters said,
"If you want to be given everything,
give everything up,"
they weren't using empty phrases.
Only in being lived by the Tao
can you be truly yourself.

1. *"The Master, by residing in the Tao, sets an example for all beings." What does that mean?*
2. *How do you succeed in everything?*
3. *"If you want to be given everything, give everything up." How do you do that?*
4. *How can you be truly yourself?*

COMMENTARY: Everything comes from where? If you want something, it is far away. If you don't want it, it is already in front of you.

| 258. *Open Yourself*

If you open yourself to the Tao,
you are at one with the Tao
and you can embody it completely.
If you open yourself to insight,
you are at one with insight
and you can use it completely.
If you open yourself to loss,
you are at one with loss
and you can accept it completely.

Open yourself to the Tao,
then trust your natural responses;
and everything will fall into place.

1. *How do you open yourself to the Tao?*
2. *How do you open yourself to insight?*
3. *If you are already at one with the Tao, why is it necessary to open yourself to the Tao?*

COMMENTARY: The Tao is always in front of you, but if you have eyes, you cannot see it. If you have ears, you cannot hear it. If you have a mouth, you cannot say, "Tao." Be careful, be careful.

| 259. *Your Job*

If you want to accord with the Tao,
just do your job, then let go.

1. *The Tao and your job, are they the same or different?*
2. *If you are the same as your job, how do you let go?*
3. *If you are different from your job, how do you let go?*

COMMENTARY: What is "Tao?" What is "Not-Tao?" Open your mouth and you go to hell; close your mouth and you lose your life. Do you see? Do you hear?

| 260. *The Four Great Powers*

There was something formless and perfect
before the universe was born.
It is serene. Empty.
Solitary. Unchanging.
Infinite. Eternally present.
It is the mother of the universe.
For lack of a better name,
I call it the Tao.

It flows through all things,
inside and outside, and returns
to the origin of all things.

The Tao is great.
The universe is great.
Earth is great.
Man is great.
These are the four great powers.

Man follows the earth.
Earth follows the universe.
The universe follows the Tao.
The Tao follows only itself.

1. *In serene emptiness, how was the universe born?*
2. *"I call it the Tao." Before I, before Tao – what?*
3. *"The Tao follows only itself." What does that mean?*

COMMENTARY: Everything is from the Tao; where does the Tao come from? Open your mouth, you lose your life; close your mouth, you become a rock. Do you see the Tao? Do you hear the Tao?

| 261. *Great Secret*

Thus the Master is available to all people
and doesn't reject anyone.
He is ready to use all situations
and doesn't waste anything.
This is called embodying the light.

What is a good man but a bad man's teacher?
What is a bad man but a good man's job?
If you don't understand this, you will get lost,
however intelligent you are.
It is the great secret.

1. *"He is ready to use all situations . . ." How do you use all situations?*
2. *What does it mean to embody the light?*
3. *Are good and bad the same or different?*
4. *What is the great secret?*

COMMENTARY: The Tao makes everything, and the Tao takes everything away. If you attain the Tao, you attain everything, and freedom from life and death.

262. The Center of the Circle

There is a time for being ahead,
a time for being behind;
a time for being in motion,
a time for being at rest;
a time for being vigorous,
a time for being exhausted;
a time for being safe,
a time for being in danger.

The Master sees things as they are,
without trying to control them.
She lets them go their own way,
and resides at the center of the circle.

1. *Who made time?*
2. *The Master and her own way: How are they different?*
3. *Where is the center of the circle?*

COMMENTARY: The Master uses the Tao to make everything. If there is no Tao, what can she make? Pay attention, pay attention!

263. Centered in the Tao

The Tao can't be perceived.
Smaller than an electron,
it contains uncountable galaxies.

If powerful men and women
could remain centered in the Tao,
all things would be in harmony.
The world would become a paradise.
All people would be at peace,
and the law would be written in their hearts.

When you have names and forms,
know that they are provisional.
When you have institutions,

know where their functions should end.
Knowing when to stop,
you can avoid any danger.

All things end in the Tao
as rivers flow into the sea.

1. *The Tao can't be perceived and is smaller than an electron.
   How do you know that?*
2. *How do you remain centered in the Tao?*
3. *"All things end in the Tao." What does this mean?*

COMMENTARY: The woman attains the Tao and gets
happiness. The man loses the Tao and gets suffering as big as
Sumi Mountain.

264. Make Everything

The great Tao flows everywhere.
All things are born from it,
yet it doesn't create them.
It pours itself into its work,
yet it makes no claim.
It nourishes infinite worlds,
yet it doesn't hold onto them.
Since it is merged with all things
and hidden in their hearts,
it can be called humble.

1. *"The great Tao flows everywhere." What does this mean?*
2. *"It pours itself into its work, yet it makes no claim." What
   does this mean?*
3. *How do you support everything?*

COMMENTARY: The ground supports the mountains, trees,
human beings, animals – everything. Space supports the earth.
What thing supports space? If you find that, then you
understand that you have two legs.

265. Free of Desire

The Tao never does anything,
yet through it all things are done.

If powerful men and women
could center themselves in it,
the whole world would be transformed
by itself, in its natural rhythms.
People would be content
with their simple, everyday lives,
in harmony, and free of desire.

When there is no desire,
all things are at peace.

1. *Sometimes the Tao makes everything. But here it never does anything. Which one is correct?*
2. *Tao, Man, and Woman. What kind of relationship?*
3. *The Tao is everything, desire and peace. Is that the Tao?*

COMMENTARY: The wife wants a baby. The husband doesn't want a baby. Who understands the Tao? The wife? The husband? Put it all down. Go drink tea.

266. When the Tao Is Lost

When the Tao is lost, there is goodness.
When goodness is lost, there is morality.
When morality is lost, there is ritual.
Ritual is the husk of true faith,
the beginning of chaos.

Therefore the Master concerns himself
with the depths and not the surface,
with the fruit and not the flower.
He has no will of his own.
He dwells in reality,
and lets all illusions go.

1. *How is the Tao lost and how does goodness appear?*
2. *How does the Master concern himself with the depths, not the surface?*
3. *Let all illusions go, then what?*

COMMENTARY: Where does the Tao come from? Where does the Tao go? The baby is crying. He wants milk.

267. *In Harmony with the Tao*

In harmony with the Tao,
the sky is clear and spacious,
the earth is solid and full,
all creatures flourish together,
content with the way they are,
endlessly repeating themselves,
endlessly renewed.

When man interferes with the Tao,
the sky becomes filthy,
the earth becomes depleted,
the equilibrium crumbles,
creatures become extinct.

The Master views the parts with compassion,
because he understands the whole.
His constant practice is humility.
He doesn't glitter like a jewel
but lets himself be shaped by the Tao,
as rugged and common as a stone.

1. *How can you be in harmony with the Tao?*
2. *How does man interfere with the Tao?*
3. *How does the Master view the parts with compassion?*

COMMENTARY: Clouds in the southern sky, rain in the northern skies. The farmer is busy working in the garden, and the children return home after school.

268. The Being of Non-Being

Return is the movement of the Tao.
Yielding is the way of the Tao.

All things are born of being.
Being is born of non-being.

1. *"Yielding is the way of the Tao." What does this mean?*
2. *"Being is born of non-being." What does this mean?*

COMMENTARY: The earth goes around the sun. The moon goes around the earth. The stars are always shining in the sky, but at night they are bright while during the daytime they cannot be seen.

269. Foolish Man

When a superior man hears of the Tao,
he immediately begins to embody it.
When an average man hears of the Tao,
he half believes it, half doubts it.
When a foolish man hears of the Tao,
he laughs out loud.
If he didn't laugh,
it wouldn't be the Tao.

Thus it is said:
The path into the light seems dark,
the path forward seems to go back,
the direct path seems long,
true power seems weak,
true purity seems tarnished,
true steadfastness seems changeable,
true clarity seems obscure,
the greatest art seems unsophisticated,
the greatest love seems indifferent,
the greatest wisdom seems childish.

The Tao is nowhere to be found.
Yet it nourishes and completes all things.

1. *Superior man, average man, and foolish man. Which one is the best man?*
2. *"The path into the light seems dark . . . true power seems weak." Do those opposites come from the Tao or not?*
3. *"The Tao is nowhere to be found." Then where is it?*

COMMENTARY: The airplane has complete freedom of movement in the sky yet cannot land wherever it wants. The superior man keeps a mind which is clear like space. He can do anything yet his mind's function is meticulous, meticulous, complete, complete.

270. Where Was the Tao Born?

The Tao gives birth to One.
One gives birth to Two.
Two gives birth to Three.
Three gives birth to all things.

All things have their backs to the female
and stand facing the male.
When male and female combine,
all things achieve harmony.

Ordinary men hate solitude.
But the Master makes use of it,
embracing his aloneness, realizing
he is one with the whole universe.

1. *"The Tao gives birth to One." Where was the Tao born?*
2. *"Three gives birth to all things." Then are good and bad also from the Tao?*
3. *All things are already harmonized and complete. Who broke harmony and completeness?*

COMMENTARY: 1, 2, 3, 4, 5; 5, 4, 3, 2, 1. Where do these numbers come from? Who made these numbers? Attaining this point, you can use any number without hindrance.

271. *The Tao Speaks for Itself*

True perfection seems imperfect,
yet it is perfectly itself.
True fullness seems empty,
yet it is fully present.

True straightness seems crooked.
True wisdom seems foolish.
True art seems artless.

The Master allows things to happen.
She shapes events as they come.
She steps out of the way
and lets the Tao speak for itself.

1. *"True perfection seems imperfect, yet it is perfectly itself."
   Why?*
2. *"True fullness seems empty, yet it is fully present." Does the
   present exist?*
3. *How does the Master let the Tao speak for itself?*

COMMENTARY: Originally, nothing. Who made past,
present, and future? If you don't make anything, you will see
and hear clearly. Then everything is your original face.

272. *No Mind of Her Own*

The Master has no mind of her own.
She works with the mind of the people.

She is good to people who are good.
She is also good to people who aren't good.
This is true goodness.

She trusts people who are trustworthy.
She also trusts people who aren't trustworthy.
This is true trust.

The Master's mind is like space.
People don't understand her.

169

They look to her and wait.
She treats them like her own children.

1. *If the Master has no mind of her own, how does she work with the mind of the people?*
2. *What is "true goodness?"*
3. *"The Master's mind is like space." What does this mean?*

COMMENTARY: The sky never says, "I am the truth." The earth never says, "I am correct." The water never says, "I am the correct way." If you make something, you hinder something. It you don't make anything, you are free.

| 273. *Where Does He Go?*

The Master gives himself up
to whatever the moment brings.
He knows that he is going to die,
and he has nothing left to hold on to:
no illusions in his mind,
no resistance in his body.
He doesn't think about his actions;
they flow from the core of his being.
He holds nothing back from life;
therefore he is ready for death,
as a man is ready for sleep
after a good day's work.

1. *"The Master gives himself up to whatever the moment brings." What does this mean?*
2. *"He knows he is going to die . . ." Then where will he go?*
3. *"He doesn't think about his actions." How do they flow from the core of his being?*
4. *How does he hold nothing back from life?*

COMMENTARY: The Master can do anything. But before he was born, where did he come from? Where does he go after he dies? The sky is always blue, water always flowing.

274. True Knowledge

Not-knowing is true knowledge,
presuming to know is a disease.
First realize you are sick;
then you can move toward health.

The Master is her own physician.
She has healed herself of all knowing.
Thus she is truly whole.

1. *"Not-knowing is true knowledge." What is true knowledge?*
2. *If the Master is her own doctor, how will she fix the world's sickness?*
3. *"Thus she is truly whole." What does she understand?*

COMMENTARY: Sugar is sweet, salt is salty. If you have no tongue, what do you taste? The child likes candy.

275. Good Man and Bad Man

The Tao is the center of the universe,
the good man's treasure,
the bad man's refuge.

Honors can be bought with fine words,
respect can be won with good deeds;
but the Tao is beyond all value,
and no one can achieve it.

Thus, when a new leader is chosen,
don't offer to help him
with your wealth or your expertise.
Offer instead
to teach him about the Tao.

Why did the ancient Masters esteem the Tao?
Because, being one with the Tao,
when you seek, you find;
and when you make a mistake, you are
forgiven.
That is why everybody loves it.

1. *The Tao is the center of the universe and has no good or bad.*
   Good men and bad men come from where?
2. *How do you teach about the Tao?*
3. *How can you be one with the Tao?*

COMMENTARY: The sun rises in the east and the whole universe is bright. Red comes, red appears; white comes, white. The sun sets in the West and the whole world is dark – you cannot see anything. But if your mind is bright, your direction appears clearly in front of you.

276. True Nature

The ancient Masters
didn't try to educate the people,
but kindly taught them to not-know.

When they think they know the answers,
people are difficult to guide.
When they know that they don't know,
people can find their own way.

1. *Who are the ancient Masters?*
2. *"When they know that they don't know . . ." What does that*
   mean?
3. *What is your own way?*

COMMENTARY: The dog is barking, "Woof, woof." The cat is crying, "Meow, meow." The bird is singing, "Chirp, chirp." What is your true speech? If you don't understand, go ask your mother.

277. Avoid Being Clever or Rich

If you want to learn how to govern,
avoid being clever or rich.
The simplest pattern is the clearest.
Content with an ordinary life,
you can show all people the way
back to their own true nature.

1. *How does the Master avoid being clever or rich?*
2. *How can you be content with an ordinary life?*
3. *How old is true nature?*

COMMENTARY: In spring, many flowers; summer is very hot. Autumn has many fruits, and in winter there is a lot of snow. Which one do you like? If you have like and dislike, the four seasons will kill you. Be careful, be careful!

278. Always at Ease

The Tao is always at ease.
It overcomes without competing,
answers without speaking a word,
arrives without being summoned,
accomplishes without a plan.

Its net covers the whole universe.
And though its meshes are wide,
it doesn't let a thing slip through.

1. *The Tao is always at ease. What kind of ease?*
2. *How do you answer without speaking a word?*
3. *This world is originally nothing. What thing slips through?*

COMMENTARY: Everything comes from the Tao; where does the Tao come from? Your mouth? Your eyes? Your nose? Your tongue? Your body? When your body disappears, where does the Tao go?

279. *True Words*

True words aren't eloquent;
eloquent words aren't true.
Wise men don't need to prove their point;
men who need to prove their point aren't wise.

The Master has no possessions.
The more he does for others,
the happier he is.
The more he gives to others,
the wealthier he is.

The Tao nourishes by not forcing.
By not dominating, the Master leads.

1. *What are "true words?"*
2. *If the Master has no possessions, how can he help all beings?*
3. *"The Tao nourishes by not forcing." Where does it come from?*

COMMENTARY: The Master is everywhere, the Master is nowhere. Which one is correct? The baby is crying, so you must give her some milk. The old man is sick; you must give him some acupuncture.

280. *Joju's Dog*

A monk asked Zen Master Joju, "Does a dog have Buddha-nature?" Joju replied, "Mu!" (No)

1. *The Buddha said that everything has Buddha-nature. Joju said that a dog has no Buddha-nature. Which one is correct?*
2. *Joju said, "Mu!" What does this mean?*
3. *I ask you, does a dog have Buddha-nature?*

COMMENTARY: Silence is better than holiness, so opening your mouth is a big mistake. But if you use this mistake to save all beings, this is Zen.

281. Pai Chang's Fox

Whenever Master Pai Chang gave a Dharma talk, an old layman would come to listen, and would leave with the monks when the talk was finished. One day, he remained behind, and the Master asked him, "Who are you?"

"I am not a human being," the old man replied. "In the distant past, in the time of Mahakashyapa, I was the Master of this mountain and made a great mistake. A monk once asked me, 'Is an enlightened person subject to samsara, the wheel of cause and effect?' I replied, 'No, an enlightened person is not subject to cause and effect.' Because of this answer, I was reborn a fox for five hundred generations. Now please, Master, give me one sentence to liberate me from the fox's body. Is an enlightened person subject to samsara, the wheel of cause and effect?"

"Cause and effect are clear," Pai Chang said. Upon hearing these words, the old man got enlightenment, and bowing, said, "I am already liberated from my fox's body, which can be found in a cave on the other side of this mountain. Would you please bury it as you would a dead monk?"

The Master then had the Temple Director strike the gavel and announce that there would be a funeral for a dead monk after the midday meal. The monks wondered aloud, "What does this mean? Everyone is healthy, and no one is in the hospital. What's going on here?" After lunch, Master Pai Chang led them to a cave behind the mountain, poked out a dead fox with his staff, and had it ceremonially cremated.

In the evening, Pai Chang told the whole story. Hwang Beok immediately asked, "This old man made one word-mistake and was reborn as a fox for five hundred generations. Suppose he had not made a mistake, what would have happened then?"

"Come here and I will tell tell you." Hwang Beok then walked up to Pai Chang and slapped him. The Master clapped his hands, laughed and said, "I thought that the barbarian had a red beard, but now I see that the barbarian's beard is red."

1. "Is not subject to cause and effect" and "Cause and effect are clear." Are these statements the same or different?
2. How did the old man become free of the fox's body?
3. What kind of body would the old man have received if he did not make a mistake?
4. Why did Hwang Beok hit Master Pai Chang?
5. What is the meaning of "now I see that the barbarian's beard is red?"

COMMENTARY: Three heads and seven legs. Who controls this man? If you have a mouth, you can never control him. If you can find a rabbit's horn then controlling him is possible.

282. Guji Raises a Finger

Zen Master Guji, whenever he was questioned about anything, merely held up one finger. He had a young attendant, whom a visitor once asked, "What is your Master's Dharma?" The boy stuck up one finger. Hearing of this, Guji cut off the boy's finger with a knife. As the boy ran out screaming in pain, Guji called out to him. When the boy turned his head, Guji held up one finger. The boy was suddenly enlightened.

When Guji was about to die, he said to the assembled monks, "I attained the one-finger Zen of Cheol Ryong. I used it all throughout my life, but could not exhaust it." When he finished saying this, he died.

1. What is the meaning of Guji's raising one finger?
2. What did the boy attain?
3. If you were this boy, what could you say to Zen Master Guji?

COMMENTARY: The snake has legs and puts on socks. Who can control this snake? If you have no fingers, you can control it.

283. *Bodhidharma Has No Beard*

Master Hok Am asked, "Why does Bodhidharma have no beard?"

1. *What is Bodhidharma's original face?*
2. *Why does Bodhidharma have no beard?*

COMMENTARY: Three years after his death, Bodhidharma returned to India, carrying a stick and a shoe. He never died. Where is he now? Watch your step!

284. *Hyang Eom's "Up a Tree"*

Master Hyang Eom said, "It is like a man up a tree who is hanging from a branch by his teeth. His limbs are tied and bound, so his hands cannot grasp a bough, and his feet cannot touch the tree. Another man standing under the tree asks him, 'Why did Bodhidharma come to China?'

"If he opens his mouth to answer, he will lose his life. If he does not answer, he evades his duty and will be killed."

1. *If you are in the tree, how do you stay alive?*

COMMENTARY: "Aigo, aigo, aigo!" Who died? Your mother or your son? It appears clearly in front of you.

285. *Shakyamuni Buddha Holds Up a Flower*

Long ago on Yeong Sahn Mountain (Grdhrakuta), Shakyamuni Buddha sat down to give a Dharma talk before a vast assembly of

177

followers. After sitting several minutes in silence, he held up a flower. All were silent. Only Mahakashyapa smiled.

Shakyamuni Buddha said, "I have the all-pervading true Dharma, incomparable Nirvana, exquisite teaching of formless form. Not dependent on words, a special transmission outside the sutras, I give it to Mahakashyapa."

1. *Why did Mahakashyapa smile?*
2. *Why did the Buddha pick up the flower?*
3. *What kind of Dharma transmission was given to Mahakashyapa?*
4. *The Buddha gave his Dharma to Mahakashyapa. But what if Mahakashapa had said, "No, thank you. I already have Dharma." If you were the Buddha, what could you do?*

COMMENTARY: The flower smiles. The Buddha's face is red.

 | ## 286. *Joju's Washing the Bowls*

A monk approached Zen Master Joju and said, "I have just entered the monastery. Please teach me, Master."

"Have you had breakfast?"

"Yes, I have," replied the monk.

"Then go wash your bowls." Upon hearing this, the monk was enlightened.

1. *What did this monk attain?*
2. *If you were the monk, what could you say to Joju?*

COMMENTARY: Breakfast in the morning, lunch at noon, dinner in the evening. After the meal, do you understand your job? Then do it.

287. Gye Chung Made a Cart

Master Wol Am said to a monk, "Gye Chung made a cart, the wheels of which had a hundred spokes. Take both front and rear parts away and remove the axle. What then becomes clear?"

1. *When all the parts are taken away, what then becomes clear?*
2. *What did you attain from this kong-an?*

COMMENTARY: In the vast sky, clouds appear and disappear. Already everything is clear.

288. Dae Tong Ji Sung

A monk asked Hung Yang of Yang, "Dae Tong Ji Sung Buddha sat Zen for ten kalpas in a meditation hall. True Dharma did not appear, so he did not attain Buddhahood. Why?"
"Good question!" Hung Yang replied.
"Already he sat in the meditation hall," the monk persisted, "why did he not attain Buddhahood?"
Hung Yang said, "Because he would not become Buddha."

1. *Why did he not attain Buddhahood?*
2. *What is the meaning of "He would not become Buddha?"*

COMMENTARY: The Hwa Yen Sutra says, "Each particle has Buddha-nature, so everything already became Buddha." If someone wants to become Buddha, it's already a big mistake. Be careful!

289. Cheong Sae Is Poor

A monk named Cheong Sae said to Cho Sahn, "I am poor and destitute. Please help me, Master."

"Cheong Sae!"

"Yes, sir?" replied Cheong Sae.

"It is as if you have drunk three cups of Chung Won Baek Ka wine [a superior vintage], but you say that you have not yet wet your lips."

1. *"I am poor and destitute. Please help me, Master." What does this mean?*
2. *What is the meaning of "It is as if you have drunk three cups of Chung Won Baek Ka wine?"*
3. *"You say that you have not yet wet your lips." What does that mean?*

COMMENTARY: The dog ate Cheong Sae's mind. Running around and around, east and west.

290. Joju's Hermits

Zen Master Joju once visited a hermit and asked, "Do you have it? Do you have it?" The hermit held up his fist. "The water is too shallow to anchor here," Joju said, and continued on his way. He came upon another hermit and called out, "Do you have it? Do you have it?" This hermit, too, held up his fist. "You are free to give or take away, to kill or give life," Joju said, bowing to him.

1. *Why did Joju approve of one answer and not the other?*
2. *If you were the first monk, what could you say to Joju?*
3. *If you were the second monk, what could you say to Joju?*

COMMENTARY: Together two monks killed Joju and stuffed his body into a wine bottle.

291. Song Am Eon Calls Master

Master Song Am Eon used to call himself every day, "Master!" and would answer, "Yes?" "You must keep clear!" "Yes!!"

"Never be deceived by others, any day, any time!" "Yes! Yes!"

1. *What is the meaning of "Master!"*
2. *Song Am Eon used to call himself and answer himself. Which one is the correct master?*

COMMENTARY: Stupid, stupid! Woman's face, man's face, who understands? Wash your face, then it appears clearly.

292. Dok Sahn Carrying His Bowls

One day, Zen Master Dok Sahn entered the Dharma Room carrying his bowls. The Housemaster, Sol Bong, said, "Old Master, the bell has not yet been rung, and the drum has not yet been struck. Where are you going, carrying your bowls?" At this, Dok Sahn returned to the Master's room. Sol Bong told the Head Monk, Am Du, what had happened.

"Great Master Dok Sahn does not understand the last word," Am Du said.

Dok Sahn heard of this and sent for Am Du. "Do you not approve of me?" he demanded. Then Am Du whispered in the Master's ear. Dok Sahn was relieved.

The next day, delivering his Dharma talk from the high rostrum, Dok Sahn was really different than before. Am Du went to the front of the Dharma room, laughed loudly, clapped his hands, and said, "Great joy! The old Master has understood the last word! From now on, no one can check him."

1. *What is the last word?*
2. *What did Am Du whisper in the Master's ear?*
3. *How was the Master's speech different from before?*
4. *If you were Dok Sahn, and Sol Bong asked you, "Where are you going, carrying your bowls," how would you answer?*

COMMENTARY: Three dogs chase each other's tails in a circle, following the smell, looking for food.

293. *Nam Cheon Kills a Cat*

One morning, the monks of the Eastern and Western halls were arguing over a cat. Hearing the loud dispute as he passed, Master Nam Cheon held up the cat in one hand and a knife in the other and shouted, "You! Give me one word and I will save this cat! If you cannot, I will kill it!"

No one could answer. Finally, Nam Cheon cut the cat in two.

In the evening, when Joju returned from outside the temple, Nam Cheon told him of the incident. Joju took off his shoes, put them on his head, and walked away.

Nam Cheon said, "Alas, if you had been there, I could have saved that cat."

1. *Nam Cheon said, "Give me one word!" At that time, what could you do?*
2. *Joju put his shoe on his head. What does that mean?*
3. *Why did this high-class Zen Master break his precepts by killing the cat?*

COMMENTARY: Nam Cheon, Joju and all students are already dead. The cat says, "Meow, meow."

294. Dong Sahn's Sixty Blows

One afternoon, when Dong Sahn came to have an interview with Zen Master Un Mun, he was asked, "Where have you been recently?"

"At Sah Do, Master," Dong Sahn replied.

"Where did you stay last summer?"

"At Bo Ja Temple in Hoe Nam."

"When did you leave there?"

"On the twenty-fifth day of August," answered Dong Sahn.

"I give you sixty blows with a stick!" Un Mun exclaimed.

The next day Dong Sahn came again to Un Mun. "Yesterday, you gave me sixty blows with a stick. I don't know where my mistake is."

"You rice bag!" Un Mun cried. "Why have you been prowling around Kang Soe and Hoe Nam?" At this, Dong Sahn got enlightenment.

1. *Why did Un Mun give Dong Sahn sixty blows with a stick?*
2. *What is the meaning of prowling around Kang Soe and Hoe Nam?*
3. *Dong Sahn got enlightenment. What did he attain?*

COMMENTARY: Snow in the north, rain in the south. Somebody got enlightenment – already a big mistake. Go drink tea.

295. Bell Sound and Seven-fold Robe

The famous Chinese Zen Master Un Mun said, "This world is vast and wide; why do you put on a seven-fold robe at the sound of a bell?"

1. *"This world is vast and wide." What does that mean?*
2. *"Why do you put on a seven-fold robe at the sound of a bell?"*
3. *If you don't have a seven-fold robe, what can you do?*

COMMENTARY: Your mind and this world, which one is bigger? Open your mouth and you cannot find your direction. Close your mouth and you lose your direction. At the sound of the bell, go to the Dharma Room.

296. The National Teacher Calls Three Times

The National Teacher called out to his attendant three times, and the attendant answered three times.

The National Teacher said, "I thought I had deserted you, but originally, you deserted me."

1. *One time is enough. Why call three times?*
2. *"I thought I had deserted you, but originally, you deserted me." What does that mean?*
3. *If you were the attendant, what could you do?*

COMMENTARY: The grandfather loves his grandson. The grandson tolerates his grandfather; he only wants candy.

297. Dong Sahn's Three Pounds of Flax

When Zen Master Dong Sahn was asked by a monk, "What is Buddha?" he answered, "Three pounds of flax."

1. *What is Buddha?*
2. *What does "Three pounds of flax" mean?*

3. *If you were the monk, what could you say?*

COMMENTARY: Big mistake, big mistake. Dong Sahn doesn't understand three pounds of flax. But three pounds of flax understand Dong Sahn's two eyes.

298. *Everyday Mind Is the True Way*

Joju asked Zen Master Nam Cheon, "What is the true way?"

"Everyday mind is the true way."

"Then should I try to keep it or not?"

"If you try to keep it, you are already mistaken."

"But if I do not try, how can I understand the true way?"

Nam Cheon said, "The true way is not dependent on understanding or not understanding. Understanding is illusion; not understanding is blankness. If you completely attain the true way of not thinking, it is like space, clear and void. So, why do you make right and wrong?" Upon hearing this, Joju suddenly got enlightenment.

1. *What is the true way?*
2. *"Everyday mind is the true way." What does this mean?*
3. *"It is like space, clear and void." What does this mean?*
4. *What did Joju attain?*
5. *If you were Joju, what could you say?*

COMMENTARY: Not eating for three days, you only desire food. Walking in the desert, you only desire water. The baby cries, and wants to see its mother. Everything is clear. Many stars in the sky, many trees on the mountainside.

299. A Man of Great Strength

Zen Master Son Won said, "Why is it that a man of great strength cannot lift his leg?"

Again he said, "It is not with his tongue that he speaks."

1. *Why is that a man of great strength cannot lift his leg?*
2. *How does he speak without his tongue?*
3. *Who is a man of great strength?*

COMMENTARY: You ate too much, so you must exercise. If you are thirsty, find a well. If you are tired, go to sleep.

300. Un Mun's Shit-Stick

A monk asked Zen Master Un Mun, "What is Buddha?"

Un Mun said, "Dry shit on a stick!"

1. *What is Buddha?*
2. *What is dry shit on a stick?*
3. *If you were the monk, what could you say to Un Mun?*

COMMENTARY: Un Mun's mouth smells bad. How do you remove the smell? Take him to the bathroom and rinse his mouth out.

301. Mahakashyapa's Flagpole

Ananda asked Mahakashyapa, "Buddha transmitted to you the Golden Brocade Robe. What else did he transmit to you?"

Mahakashyapa called out, "Ananda!"

"Yes, sir!"

"Knock down the flagpole in front of the gate."

1. *What else did Buddha transmit to Mahakashyapa?*
2. *Mahakashyapa called Ananda. Ananda answered. What does this call and answer mean?*
3. *"Knock down the flagpole in front of the gate." What does this mean?*
4. *If you were Ananda, and Mahakashyapa said, "Knock down the flagpole," what could you say?*

COMMENTARY: The sky has no clouds, but lightning hits the flagpole. Mahakashyapa and Ananda both lose their jobs.

302. Don't Think Good and Bad

The Sixth Patriarch was once pursued by the monk Hae Myung to Dae Yu Ryong. Seeing Hae Myung coming, the Patriarch laid his robe and bowl on a stone, saying, "This robe symbolizes faith: how can it be fought over? I leave it to you to take."

Hae Myung tried to pick up the robe, but it was as immovable as a mountain. He became terrified and hesitated, crying, "I have come for the Dharma, not for the robe. I beg you, please teach me, layman brother!"

The Sixth Patriarch said, "Don't think good and bad. At that time, what is Hae Myung's original face?" Hae Myung was instantly enlightened.

In tears, his entire body dripping with sweat, he bowed and asked, "Besides these secret words and meanings, is there more secret meaning?"

"What I have just told you is not secret," the Patriarch replied. "If you perceive the face of your true self, then that which is secret, you already have."

Hae Myung said, "Although at Hwang Mae Mountain I followed other monks in training, I could not understand my original face. Now, thanks to your teaching, which is clear and to the point, my understanding is like drinking water: I understand myself whether it is warm or cold. So now you are my teacher."

"If you are already like this," the Patriarch said, "then you and I are both students of the Fifth Patriarch. Take care of your true self. Only go straight."

1. *Don't think good and bad. What is your original face?*
2. *What did Hae Myung attain?*
3. *What is the secret you already have?*
4. *What is the meaning of "Only go straight?"*

COMMENTARY: The Sixth Patriarch has two eyes; Hae Myung has two ears. Each has one mouth. Together they see and hear, but their speech is different. One goes north, one goes south.

303. *Discard Speech and Words*

A monk once asked Zen Master Pung Hol, "Both speech and silence include separation and union. How can we be free and without fault?"

Pung Hol said, "I still remember Kong Nam in March. Many fragrant flowers where the partridges call."

1. *Without speech and silence, how can you answer?*
2. *How can we be free and without fault?*
3. *Where is Pung Hol's mistake?*

COMMENTARY: Open your mouth, there is no tongue. Open your eyes, there is no pupil. How do you fix this? You must go to Kong Nam and ask the partridges.

304. Dharma Speech of the Third Seat

Master Ang Sahn had a dream in which he went to the place where Maitreya was teaching and was given the third seat. A venerable monk struck the table with a gavel and said, "Today the talk will be given by the monk in the third seat."

Ang Sahn then stuck the table with the gavel and said, "The Dharma of Mahayana goes beyond the Four Propositions and transcends the One Hundred Negations. Listen carefully! Listen carefully!"

1. *Ang Sahn made a big mistake. Where is it?*
2. *What did you attain from this kong-an?*

COMMENTARY: This world and human life are like a dream. Two men talk about the dream. When will they wake up? Outside the house, at three o'clock in the morning, the chicken is crowing, "Cock-a-doodle-doo!"

305. Two Monks Roll Up the Blinds

Two monks visited Chung Yang Dae Poep An before a ceremony. Poep An pointed to the bamboo blinds. At this, the two monks went to the blinds and rolled them up simultaneously. Poep An said, "One has got it. One has lost it."

1. *"One has got it. One has lost it." What does this mean?*
2. *Which monk has it? Which monk lost it?*
3. *If you were one of these monks, what could you say to Poep An?*

COMMENTARY: The two monks' action is very clear. Poep An's speech is a big mistake. How do you make it correct? Do you understand Poep An's age? Go ask the pine tree in front of the temple.

306. Is Not Mind, Is Not Buddha

A monk once asked Zen Master Nam Cheon, "Is there 'without-speech' Dharma for all people?"

"There is."

"What is 'without-speech' Dharma for all people?"

Nam Cheon said, "Is not mind, is not Buddha, is not anything."

1. *Is there 'without-speech Dharma' for all people?*
2. *Where is Nam Cheon's mistake?*
3. *"Is not mind, is not Buddha, is not anything." Then what is it?*

COMMENTARY: Ten thousand words, ten thousand mistakes. In complete silence, everything is clear in front of you. Just see, just hear.

307. Well-Known Yong Dam

Dok Sahn once called on Zen Master Yong Dam and stayed late into the night. Yong Dam finally said, "It is late, you should go." Dok Sahn said goodbye, lifted the curtain hanging in the doorway, and went out. Seeing that it was pitch dark, he turned back and said, "Master, it is very dark outside."

Yong Dam lit a rice-paper candle and handed it to him. Just as Dok Sahn was about to take it Yong Dam blew it out. At this, Dok Sahn was instantly enlightened. He bowed deeply.

Yong Dam asked, "What did you understand?"

"From now on," Dok Sahn replied, "I will believe the teachings of all Zen Masters in the world."

The next day, Zen Master Yong Dam mounted the high rostrum and declared, "Among you there is one big man whose fangs are like swords, and whose mouth is like a big blood pot. You may hit him with a stick, but he will not turn his head. Some day in the future, he will make his way to the top of a high mountain."

Dok Sahn then took out his notes and commentaries on the *Diamond Sutra* and, in front of the monastery hall, he held up a burning torch and said, "Even though one may master various profound philosophies, it is like placing a single strand of hair in the great sky. Even if one gains all the essential knowledge in the world, it is like throwing a drop of water into a deep ravine."

Then, taking up his notes and commentaries, he burned them all, and bowed gratefully.

1. *What did Dok Sahn attain?*
2. *"Among you there is one big man whose fangs are like swords, and whose mouth is like a big blood pot." Who is this man?*
3. *"From now on, I will believe the teachings of all the Zen Masters in the world." What does that mean?*
4. *What does "placing a single strand of hair in the great sky" mean?*

COMMENTARY: Nature is already teaching us everything. Why do you need all the sutras? If you attain your original face, you can throw all of the Buddha's sutras into the fire. Then your world is complete.

308. Not Wind, Not Flag

Arriving at a temple, the Sixth Patriarch came upon two monks arguing over a flag that was flapping in the wind. One said the flag was moving; the other claimed the wind was moving.

The Sixth Patriarch said, "It is not the wind; it is not the flag. It is your minds that are moving." The monks were completely stuck, and could not answer.

1. *Is the flag or the wind moving?*
2. *One monk was attached to wind. One monk was attached to flag. The Sixth Patriarch was attached to mind. How do you avoid these attachments?*
3. *Is someone had said to the Sixth Patriarch, "Your mind is also moving," how could he have responded?*

COMMENTARY: The two monks don't have a problem. The Sixth Patriarch makes a big mistake because he once said, "Originally nothing." Where is mind? Wind and flag may control the two monks, but mind controls the Sixth Patriarch.

309. Mind Is Buddha

Tae Mae once asked Zen Master Ma Jo, "What is Buddha?"

"Mind is Buddha," Ma Jo responded.

1. *What is Buddha?*
2. *What is mind?*
3. *Mind and Buddha, are they the same or different?*

COMMENTARY: No Ma Jo, no monk, no Buddha, no mind, then what? Do you see the sky? Do you see the tree? Already you understand. Put it all down.

310. No Mind, No Buddha

A monk once asked Zen Master Ma Jo, "What is Buddha?"

Ma Jo answered, "No mind, no Buddha."

1. *What is Buddha?*
2. *Show me "No mind, no Buddha."*
3. *No mind, no Buddha, then what?*

COMMENTARY: The rocks don't want Buddha or mind. The tree doesn't want truth or correct way. They only do it. They attain it.

311. Joju Sees Through the Old Woman

A journeying monk asked an old woman he met on the road, "How do I get to Tae Sahn?"

She said, "Go straight ahead." After he took three or four steps, the woman said, "You are a very good monk, but you must go *this* way," and pointed in another direction.

Later, the monk told Zen Master Joju about it. Joju said, "I will go and see through this old woman."

The next day, he went to the place where the monk encountered the woman and asked her the same question. The old woman gave the same answer. Upon his return, Joju told the assembly, "I have completely seen through the old woman from Tae Sahn."

1. *Why did the old woman test the monk?*
2. *When Joju tested this old woman, did he have mind or not?*
3. *What does "I have completely seen through the old woman from Tae Sahn" mean?*

COMMENTARY: Joju has eyes, ears, nose, tongue, and body, but he has no bone. How does he come down from Tae Sahn and return to Tae Sahn? The old woman has no eyes, no mouth, no hands; how did she point the way to Tae Sahn? That's very funny! Ha, ha, ha!!

312. An Outer Path Question to the Buddha

An "outer path"* man once asked the Buddha, "I do not ask for words; I do not ask for silence." The Buddha changed position to sit correctly.

The outer path man praised him, saying, "Buddha, your great compassion has opened my mind, taken away the cloud of ignorance, and let me get enlightened." He bowed to the Buddha and departed.

Then Ananda asked the Buddha, "What did he get, and why did he praise you?"

The Buddha said, "He is like a high-spirited horse, which starts at the shadow of a whip."

1. *I do not ask for words or silence. What can you do?*
2. *The Buddha changed positions. What does this mean?*
3. *What did the outer path man attain?*
4. *"He is like a high-spirited horse, which starts at the shadow of a whip." What does that mean?*

COMMENTARY: The tree, the water, the ground and the sky have no speech, but they teach us completeness. If you don't understand the correct way, truth, and correct life, you must ask the sun and the moon.

313. Cognition Is Not the Path

Zen Master Nam Cheon said, "Mind is not Buddha; cognition is not the path."

1. *What is cognition?*
2. *What is the path?*

---

*The term "outer path" refers to non-Buddhists or Buddhist heretics. It also refers to distinguished non-Buddhists who would visit the Buddha to test him with difficult questions.

3. *Mind and Buddha, are they the same or different?*

COMMENTARY: The cat understands cat's job, the dog understands dog's job, the chicken understands chicken's job. Human beings don't understand human being's job. What are you doing right now? Just do it.

314. *Chong Nyo's Soul Leaves*

Oh Jo asked a monk, "Chong Nyo and her soul are separated: Which is the true one?"

1. *Chong Nyo and her soul, are they the same or different?*
2. *Chong Nyo and her soul are separated. Which is the true one?*

COMMENTARY: Anger, ignorance, desire, happiness, sadness. Which one is the true mind? If you have no mind, where do they go? One appears, two appears. Two appears, ten thousand things appear. One disappears, everything disappears.

315. *Meeting a Master on the Road*

Zen Master Oh Jo said, "If you meet a master on the road, you don't need words or silence. Now tell me, how do you greet him?"

1, *What is a master's job?*
2. *How do you greet a master on the road?*

COMMENTARY: The tree understands the weather. The mountain understands the season. All animals understand their situation and their actions. Only human beings are stupid. In spring, the grass is green. In winter, the snow is white.

316. The Cypress Tree in the Front Garden

A monk asked Zen Master Joju, "Why did Bodhidharma come to China?"

Joju said, "The cypress tree in the front garden."

1. *Who is Bodhidharma?*
2. *Why did Bodhidharma come to China?*
3. *What does "The cypress tree in the front garden" mean?*
4. *If you were the monk and Joju gave you this answer, what could you have done?*

COMMENTARY: Hard training, very difficult job for Bodhidharma. His "do it" opened many peoples' eyes but he lost his body. Then three years after he died, he found his body and went to India. Where is he now? The sky is blue; the pine tree is green.

317. A Water Buffalo Passes Through a Window

Zen Master Oh Jo said, "It is like a water buffalo passing through a window. Its head, horns, and four legs have already passed through. Why is it that its tail cannot?"

1. *Where is the water buffalo?*
2. *How did the water buffalo's head, horns, and legs pass through the window?*
3. *Why can't the tail pass through?*

COMMENTARY: The water buffalo's tail killed all Buddhas, killed all teachers and all beings. Where is the buffalo's tail? Do you see it? Are you holding it? It has already passed.

318. Un Mun's Trip on a Word

A monk said to Zen Master Un Mun, "Clear light shines serenely over the whole universe ..." when the master interrupted him to ask, "is that Chan Jul Su Jae's speech?"

"Yes, sir."

"You have tripped on a word!"

Years later, Master Sa Shim picked up these words and said, "Tell me! Where is the place that this monk has tripped on a word?"

1. *"Clear light shines serenely over the whole universe." What does that mean?*
2. *Why did Un Mun say, "You have tripped on a word"?*
3. *Where is the place that this monk has tripped on a word?*

COMMENTARY: The crow calls, "Caw, caw." The dog barks, "Woof, woof." Human beings open their mouths and many words appear. Big mistake! Do you understand Un Mun's mistake? Go drink tea.

319. Kicking Over the Urine Bottle

Before he became a Zen Master, Wi Sahn studied at Pai Chang's monastery, where he was Housemaster. At that time, Pai Chang wanted to choose an Abbot for Dai Wi Monastery. He told the Head Monk and assembled students, "I have a test for all of you. The one who passes this test will be sent." Then Pai Chang picked up a urine bottle, placed it on the floor, and said, "This must not be called a urine bottle. What do you call it?"

The Head Monk replied, "It cannot be called a wooden block."

Pai Chang then asked Wi Sahn, who only kicked over the bottle and left.

Pai Chang laughed and said, "The Head Monk has been defeated by Wi Sahn." Because of this, Wi Sahn was sent to open the monastery.

1. *This must not be called a urine bottle. What do you call it?*
2. *Where is the Head Monk's mistake?*
3. *Why did Wi Sahn kick over the urine bottle?*

COMMENTARY: Wi Sahn is not good, not bad. Too wild, he must keep a clear mind. Are his hands on vacation?

320. Bodhidharma's Rest Mind

Bodhidharma sat facing the wall. The Second Patriarch, standing in the snow, cut off his arm and said, "My mind cannot rest. Please, Teacher, rest my mind."

Bodhidharma replied, "Bring me your mind, and I will put it at rest."

The Second Patriarch said, "I cannot find my mind."

Bodhidharma replied, "I have already given your mind rest."

1. *Do you have a mind?*
2. *At that time, what is the Second Patriarch's unrest mind?*
3. *Where did the Second Patriarch's mind go?*
4. *What is rest mind?*

COMMENTARY: Very stupid of Bodhidharma. Why did he sit for nine years? Does he have a mind or not? If he has no mind, he has already lost his life. What did the Second Patriarch attain? If you understand that, go drink tea.

321. A Woman Comes Out of Samadhi

無相
三昧

Long ago, Manjushri went to a gathering of all the Buddhas. Everyone returned to their seats, but one woman remained, seated near Shakyamuni Buddha, deep in samadhi.

Manjushri asked the Buddha, "Why can a woman sit so close to you, and I cannot?"

The Buddha told him, "Wake her up from samadhi and ask her yourself."

Manjushri walked around the woman three times and snapped his fingers. Then he put her in the palm of his hand, carried her to heaven, and used transcendent energy on her, but he still could not wake her up.

The Buddha said, "Even if a hundred Manjushris appeared, they also would not be able to wake her up. Down below, past twelve hundred million countries, is Ma Myung Bosal. He will be able to wake her up from samadhi." Immediately, Ma Myung Bosal emerged from the earth and bowed to the Buddha, who gave him the command. Ma Myung walked in front of the woman and snapped his fingers only once. At this, the woman woke from samadhi and stood up from her seat.

1. What is deep samadhi?
2. Why was a high-class Bodhisattva not able to wake the woman, while a low-class one could?
3. After the woman came out of samadhi, what became clear?

COMMENTARY: Head cannot hold a pen, eyes cannot hear a sound, mouth cannot see the clear sky. Man cannot have a baby. Hands have hands' job, legs have legs' job. Understand your correct job. When the rooster crows in the morning the body wakes up.

322. Su Sahn's Chukpi*

 Master Su Sahn held up his chukpi to an assembly of monks, saying, "If you say 'chukpi,' you touch it. If you say 'not chukpi,' you betray it. You! Tell me! What do you call it?"

1. *What do you call it?*
2. *Someone in the assembly answered correctly. If you were Su Sahn, what could you do?*

COMMENTARY: Originally no name, no form. One mind appeared, name and form appeared. If you are attached to name and form, you cannot get out of hell. Attaining the correct function of name and form, you become Buddha.

323. Pa Cho's Zen Stick

Zen Master Pa Cho said to the assembly, "If you have a Zen stick, I will give one to you. If you do not have a Zen stick, I will take it away from you."

1. *How could you answer?*
2. *If you do not have a Zen stick, how can Pa Cho take it away from you?*

COMMENTARY: All animals understand their correct way and correct action. Only human beings remain ignorant. The rabbit likes carrots, the mouse likes cheese.

---

*A *chukpi* is a wooden clapper stick used to signal the beginning and end of meditation periods and formal meals.

324. Who Is This?

The Patriarch Dong Sahn Yon Sa said, "Shakyamuni Buddha and Mi Rok Bosal are servants of another. Tell me, who is this?"

1. *Who is this?*
2. *Are the Buddha's, Mi Rok Bosal's, and this other's job different?*

COMMENTARY: If you don't make anything, the whole world is yours. If you make something, you are already dead. If you want to meet the Buddha, go to the kitchen. If you want to see Mi Rok Bosal, go to the bathroom.

325. Bodhidharma's "No Holiness Is Clear Like Space"

Emperor Wu of Liang asked the great Master Bodhidharma, "What is the highest meaning of the holy truths?"

"No holiness is clear like space."

"Who is facing me?"

"Don't know."

The Emperor became disconcerted.

Bodhidharma left Liang, crossed the Yangtse River and entered the kingdom of Wei. Later the Emperor brought this exchange up with Master Chih and questioned him about it. Master Chih asked, "Does Your Majesty know who this man is?"

"No, I don't know."

"He is the Avalokiteshvara Bodhisattva, transmitting the Buddha Mind Seal."

Hearing this, the Emperor was deeply chagrined, and wished to send an emissary to invite Bodhidharma to return. But Master Chih told him, "Your Majesty, don't say that you will send someone to fetch him back. Even if everyone in the whole country were to go after him, still he would not return."

1. What does "No holiness is clear like space" mean?
2. What does "Don't know" mean?
3. Who is Avalokiteshvara Bodhisattva?
4. If everyone goes after Bodhidharma, why won't he return?

COMMENTARY: The Emperor understands Bodhidharma. Bodhidharma doesn't understand the Emperor.
Bodhidharma's "don't know" swallowed the whole universe. How do you get out? Open your eyes and ears. Bodhidharma sat in Sorim for nine years.

 ## 326. *Master Ma Jo Is Unwell*

The great Zen Master Ma Jo was unwell. The temple Housemaster asked him, "Master, how has your venerable health been lately?"
        The great Master said, "Sun-face Buddha, moon-face Buddha."

1. What does "Sun-face Buddha, moon-face Buddha" mean?
2. No sun-face Buddha, no moon-face Buddha, then what?

COMMENTARY: The head faces the sky, the two faces face the ground. Spring comes, many flowers; winter comes, much snow. The child likes fire.

  ## 327. *Un Mun's "Every Day Is a Good Day"*

Zen Master Un Mun, instructing an assembly of monks, said, "Don't ask me before the fifteenth day of the month (Borom). After Borom, you must bring me one word." He then answered himself, saying, "Every day is a good day."

1. *What does "Every day is a good day" mean?*
2. *Who made every day?*

COMMENTARY: Time passes like an arrow. Thinking appears, yesterday and today appear. Thinking disappears, all days disappear. Is this a good day or a bad day? Look at the sky, always blue.

328. *Ministry President Ch'en Sees Tzu Fu*

Ch'en Ts'ao went to see Zen Master Tzu Fu. When Tzu Fu saw him coming, he immediately drew a circle.

Ch'en Ts'ao said, "This disciple, coming like this, is already not dependent on anything. Why, even more, do you make a circle?"

Fu immediately closed the door.

Hsueh Tou said, "Ch'en Ts'ao only has one eye."

1. *Tzu Fu made a circle. What does that mean?*
2. *If Ch'en Ts'ao had two eyes, what would he have done?*

COMMENTARY: The earth spins around on its axis and rotates around the sun. Winter, spring, summer and fall also go around. If your mind goes around and around, what do you get? Put it down – just see, just hear. Just do it!

329. *Chi Am's Eyebrows*

At the end of the summer retreat, Zen Master Chi Am said to the assembly, "All summer long I've been speaking to you, brothers. Look! Does Chi Am have eyebrows?"

Bo Bok said, "Making a thief. A coward's mind."

Jang Gyeong said, "Grown."

Un Mun said, "Barrier."

1. *Which is the correct answer?*
2. *If you were there, how would you answer?*
3. *Form is emptiness, emptiness form. Are eyebrows form or emptiness?*

COMMENTARY: The clear mirror has no likes or dislikes. Red comes, red; white comes, white. Don't use your mouth; use the clear mirror.

330. Joju's Four Gates

A monk asked Zen Master Joju, "What is Joju?"
"East gate, west gate, south gate, north gate."

1. *What is Joju?*
2. *What is "East gate, west gate, south gate, north gate"?*

COMMENTARY: Joju's original face appears very clearly, but without his eyes, ears, nose, tongue and body. Which one is the true Joju? If you want to understand the true Joju, ask the pine tree.

331. Muk Ju's Imposter

Zen Master Muk Ju asked a monk, "Where have you just come from?"
The monk immediately shouted "KATZ!"
"You have shouted at this old monk once," Muk Ju said.
Again the monk shouted, "KATZ!"
"After tree or four shouts, then what?" The monk had no words. Muk Ju then hit him and said, "You imposter!"

1. *What does "KATZ!" mean?*
2. *Where is the monk's mistake?*
3. *If you were monk, how could you make it correct?*

COMMENTARY: KATZ + KATZ + KATZ = how many pounds? Open your mouth, the Buddha's mother appears. Close your mouth, the whole universe disappears. Which one do you like?

332. Pa Nung's Snow in a Silver Bowl

A monk asked Zen Master Pa Nung, "What is the school of Kanadeva?"*

"Piling up snow in a silver bowl," Pa Nung replied.

1. *What is the school of Kanadeva?*
2. *"Piling up snow in a silver bowl." What does that mean?*
3. *No snow, no bowl, then what?*

COMMENTARY: What you see and what you hear are your true friends.

333. Gyeong Cheong's Man in the Weeds

A monk said to Zen Master Gyeong Cheong, "I am pecking out. Please, Master, peck in."

"Are you alive or not?"

"If I were not alive, people would jeer at me," the monk replied.

"You, too, are a man in the weeds."

1. *What do "pecking out" and "pecking in" mean?*
2. *Where is the monk's mistake?*
3. *How can you answer, "Are you alive or not?"*

---

*Kanadeva is the fifteenth Patriarch.

COMMENTARY: Clapping hands three times, "Wonderful, wonderful, wonderful!" The baby chick says, "Good morning, how are you?"

334. Baek Jang's "Sitting Alone on Ta Hsiung Peak"

A monk asked Zen Master Baek Jang, "What is the commendable affair?"

Baek Jang said, "Sitting alone on Ta Hsiung Peak."

The monk bowed. Then Baek Jang hit him.

1. *What is the commendable affair?*
2. *What is "sitting alone on Ta Hsiung Peak?"*
3. *Why did Baek Jang hit the monk?*
4. *If you were this monk, what could you do?*

COMMENTARY: Be careful! Don't attach to words. One action is better than ten thousand words.

335. Un Mun's "Body Exposed in the Golden Wind"

A monk once asked Zen Master Un Mun, "How is it when the tree withers and the leaves fall?"

Un Mun replied, "Body exposed in the golden wind."

1. *How is it when the tree withers and the leaves fall?*
2. *"Body exposed in the golden wind." What does this mean?*
3. *No body, no wind, then what?*

COMMENTARY: If you understand the weather outside, you will know what clothes to wear. The sun is far away, and the wind is strong.

336. *Joju's Big Radishes*

A monk asked Zen Master Joju, "Master, I heard
that you have personally seen Zen Master Nam
Cheon. Is this true or not?"

"Chen Chou* produces big radishes," Joju
replied.

1. *Are Nam Cheon and Joju the same or different?*
2. *Who is Nam Cheon?*
3. *"Chen Chou produces big radishes." What does that mean?*

COMMENTARY: Joju is more powerful than God. Nam
Cheon becomes a radish; the radish is bigger than Joju, and
falls down on his body. Joju is shouting, "Help! Help!"

337. *Lin Chi's "Buddhism's Great Meaning"*

Jeong Sang Joa asked Zen Master Lin Chi,
"What is Buddhism's Great Meaning?" Lin Chi
instantly came down off his meditation seat,
grabbed Jeong San Joa, gave him a slap, and
then pushed him away.

Jeong Sang Joa stood there utterly motionless. A monk
standing nearby said, "Jeong Sang Joa, why don't you bow?"
Just as Jeong Sang Joa bowed, he was greatly enlightened.

1. *What is Buddhism's Great Meaning?*
2. *Why did Lin Chi grab and hold Jeong Sang Joa?*
3. *What did Jeong Sang Joa attain?*

COMMENTARY: What is not Buddhism? If you find not-
Buddhism, you become Buddha. If you find Buddhism, you
become stupid. Lin Chi is very stupid. One action is
enough – why does he want three? Jeong Sang Joa
understands himself: he has two eyes and one mouth.

---

*Chen Chou is a famous city in China.

338. Manjushri's "Before Three, Three"

前
右 三三
三 三

Manjushri asked Mu Chak, "Where are you coming from?"

"The South."

"How is the Buddhist teaching being carried on in the South?"

Mu Chak said, "At the end of the Dharma (end of the world), only a few monks keep the precepts."

"How many assemblies?"

Mu Chak said, "Some three hundred, some five hundred," then asked, "How is it being carried on hereabouts?"

Manjushri replied, "Ordinary people and saints live together; dragons and snakes mix."

"How many assemblies?"

Manjushri said, "Before three, three. After three, three."

1. *If your body comes from the South, your true self comes from where?*
2. *"Before three, three. After three, three." What does this mean?*
3. *Before zero, after zero, then what?*

COMMENTARY: Stupid, stupid Manjushri. Clever, clever Mu Chak. Only a speech game – who won, who lost? Did you see Manjushri's original face? Did you see Mu Chak's original nose? Same or different? All Buddhas and eminent teachers cannot digest Manjushri's "Before three, three; after three, three."

339. Un Mun's Golden-Haired Lion

A monk asked Un Mun, "What is the pure and clear Dharma-body?"

Un Mun said, "A flowering hedge."

The monk asked, "If, when like this, how is it?"
Un Mun said, "Golden-haired lion."

1. *What is the pure and clear Dharma-body?*
2. *First, Un Mun answered, "A flowering hedge," and then "Golden-haired lion." Are they the same or different?*
3. *What does "Golden-haired lion" mean?*

COMMENTARY: Be careful! The golden-haired lion will devour you. The lion roars, "Rrrrrrrrrrr!"

340. Nam Cheon's Flowering Tree

 As the officer Yu Kan was talking with Zen Master Nam Cheon, he remarked, "Master of the teachings Gae Poep Sa once said, 'Heaven, earth, and I have the same root; ten thousand things and I are one body.' This is outrageous."

Nam Cheon pointed to a flower in the garden. He called to the officer and said, "People these days see this flowering tree as a dream."

1. *"Heaven, earth, and I have the same root." What does this mean?*
2. *"Ten thousand things and I are one body." What does this mean?*
3. *"People these days see this flowering tree as a dream." What does this mean?*

COMMENTARY: Open your mouth, big mistake. Close your mouth, the whole universe and you are never separate. Wake up! Wake up! What do you see now? What do you hear now? Go ask the dog and the cat, and they will teach you.

341. Joju's "Man of Great Death"

Zen Master Joju asked Tu Ja, "When a man of great death returns to life, how is it?"

Tu Ja replied, "Going by night is not permitted. Your must arrive in daylight."

1. *When a man of great death returns to life, how is it?*
2. *Nighttime and daytime: are they the same or different?*
3. *Why did Tu Ja say "Going by night is not permitted?"*

COMMENTARY: Coming empty-handed, going empty-handed. There is always one thing which remains clear, not dependent on life and death. Who is dead, who is alive? Life and death are like a floating cloud. If you take away the cloud in your mind, then your original face appears clearly in front of you. Nighttime is dark, daytime is bright.

342. Dong Sahn's "No Cold or Hot"

A monk asked Zen Master Dong Sahn, "When cold and hot come, how can we avoid them?"

"Why don't you go to the place where there is no cold or hot?" Dong Sahn replied.

"What is the place where there is no cold or hot?"

Dong Sahn said, "When cold, cold kills you; when hot, heat kills you."

1. *When cold and hot come, how can we avoid them?*
2. *Where is the place where there is no cold or hot?*
3. *"When cold, cold kills you; when hot, heat kills you." What is the meaning of this?*

COMMENTARY: Dong Sahn's speech is wonderful! He understands correct situation and action. Are hot and cold inside or outside? If you find the correct answer, you attain Dong Sahn's original face.

343. Ko Sahn's "Knowing How to Hit the Drum"

Zen Master Ko Sahn, instructing a group of monks, said, "Studying is called 'listening.' Cutting off study is called 'nearness.' Past these two is true passing."

A monk came forward and asked, "What is true passing?"

"Knowing how to hit the drum," Ko Sahn replied.

"And what is real truth?"

"Knowing how to hit the drum."

The monk continued, "'Mind is Buddha'–I'm not asking about this. What is 'no mind, no Buddha?'"

"Knowing how to hit the drum."

"And when a transcendent person comes, how do you receive that person?"

"Knowing how to hit the drum."

1. What is true passing?
2. What is real truth?
3. When a transcendent person comes, how do you receive that person?
4. Can you hear the sound of a stone drum?

COMMENTARY: Put down all of your speech and thinking. If you are checking, this checking will kill you. Did you hear Ko Sahn's sound of a drum? How many pounds is it? If you know that, you become Buddha's teacher.

344. Joju's "Stone Bridge, Log Bridge"

A monk said to Zen Master Joju, "For a long time, I've heard of the stone bridge of Joju, but now that I've come here, I just see a simple log bridge."

"You just see the log bridge," Joju replied, "you don't see the stone bridge."

"What is the stone bridge?"
"Asses cross, horses cross."

1. *Stone bridge, log bridge, are they the same or different?*
2. *What is a stone bridge?*
3. *Asses cross, horses cross, then what?*

COMMENTARY: The airplane flying in the sky has a direction, and a car driving down the road has a destination. The running dog and cat are better than the airplane and the car.

345. *Un Mun's Staff*

Zen Master Un Mun showed his staff to the assembly and said, "This staff has changed into a dragon and swallowed heaven and earth. Mountains, rivers, the great earth – where can they be found?"

1. *How can you make this staff a dragon?*
2. *How did this dragon swallow everything?*
3. *If this dragon swallowed everything, where can you find everything?*

COMMENTARY: Un Mun's speech is a big mistake. His hook is caught in his own mouth: who will remove this hook? Only the one who can answer the three questions will be able to remove the hook.

346. *Nam Cheon's Circle*

Three Zen Masters – Nam Cheon, Kui Jeong, and Ma Gok – went together to pay respects to National Teacher Chung. When they got halfway there, Nam Cheon drew a circle on the ground and said, "If you can speak, then let's go on." Kui Jeong sat down inside the circle, and Ma Gok curtseyed.

Nam Cheon said, "If that's so, let's not go on."
Kui Jeong asked, "What's going on in your mind?"

1. *Nam Cheon made a circle. What does it mean?*
2. *Kui Jeong sat down, and Ma Gok curtseyed. Where is their mistake?*
3. *If you were there, how would you answer?*

COMMENTARY: Nam Cheon becomes crazy like Sumi Mountain. He wants to catch a big fish but cannot get it. Kui Jeong and Ma Gok understand his mind. Nam Cheon does not understand Kui Jeong and Ma Gok's minds. Where do they go? South, north, east, west – where?

347. Geum U's "Ha Ha Ha Ha!" Great Laughing

Master Geum U, at ceremonial mealtime, would personally take the rice pail and, dancing and laughing, "Ha-ha-ha-ha," would cry, "Bodhisattvas, come eat!"

Hsueh Tou said, "Even though like that, Geum U was not good-hearted."

A monk once asked Jang Gyeong, "When the man of old said, 'Bodhisattvas, come eat!' what was his meaning?"

"Much like joyful praise at a ceremonial meal," Jang Gyeong replied.

1. *Why did Geum U personally take the rice pail and, dancing, laugh "Ha-ha-ha-ha?"*
2. *What is the meaning of "come eat?"*
3. *What is the meaning of "much like joyful praise at a ceremonial mean?"*

COMMENTARY: If you have time, go to the movies. If you are tired, go dancing. If you have nothing to do, bow to the Buddha, then the Buddha smiles at you.

348. *Un Mun's Cake*

A monk asked Un Mun, "What is talk that goes beyond Buddhas and Patriarchs?"

"Cake," Un Mun replied.

1. *What is talk that goes beyond Buddhas and Patriarchs?*
2. *What does "cake" mean?*
3. *If you were the monk, what could you say to Un Mun?*

COMMENTARY: Un Mun said, "Cake." But why only cake? If you have cookies, noodles or Coca-Cola, give them to Un Mun. Then he will approve of you.

349. *Tu Ju's "All Buddha Sounds"*

A monk asked Zen Master Tu Ju, "All sounds are the sounds of Buddha – right or wrong?"

Tu Ju said, "Right."

The monk said, "Master, doesn't your asshole make farting sounds?"

Tu Ju hit him.

Again the monk asked, "Coarse words or subtle talk, everything returns to the primary meaning – right or wrong?"

Tu Ju said, "Right."

"Then can I call you an ass, Master?"

Tu Ju hit him.

1. *Are all sounds the sounds of Buddha?*
2. *Where is Tu Ju's mistake?*
3. *Do coarse words and subtle words all return to primary meaning?*
4. *Why did Tu Ju hit the monk?*

COMMENTARY: Originally there are no words and no speech. Already a mistake. Who will make it correct? If you want to understand, ask a flower or a tree; they will give you a correct answer.

350. Joju's "Newborn Baby"

A monk asked Zen Master Joju, "Does a newborn baby have the sixth consciousness?"

"Like tossing a ball on swiftly-flowing water," Joju replied.

The monk persisted, "What is the meaning of 'Tossing a ball on swiftly-flowing water?'"

"Thoughts, thoughts, nonstop flowing."

1. *Does a newborn baby have the sixth consciousness?*
2. *Is Joju's answer correct or not?*
3. *What does "Tossing a ball on swiftly-flowing water" mean?*
4. *"Thoughts, thoughts, nonstop flowing." What does this mean?*

COMMENTARY: When the baby cries, the mother gives it milk. Joju likes the ball but the ball already killed him.

Put it all down! See clearly, hear clearly. The willow is green, the flower is red.

351. Dae Ryong's "Indestructible Dharma-Body"

A monk asked Dae Ryong, "The physical body rots away. What is the indestructible Dharma-body?"

Dae Ryong said, "The mountain flowers bloom like brocade; the valley streams are brimming blue as indigo."

1. *What is the physical body?*
2. *What is the indestructible Dharma-body?*

3. *Physical body and Dharma-body, are they the same or different?*
4. *Form is emptiness and emptiness is form. Physical body and Dharma-body, are they form or emptiness?*

COMMENTARY: Don't hold anything. Just see, just hear. Is your body Dharma-body or form body? If you are attached to form-body, you go to hell like an arrow. If you are attached to Dharma-body, you cannot find your leg. Be careful, be careful! When you are tired, just sleep. When you are thirsty, just drink. Just do it – don't make anything.

352. The Hermit of T'ung Feng Roars Like a Tiger

A monk came to the place of the hermit of T'ung Feng and asked, "If you suddenly encountered a tiger here, what then?" The hermit made a tiger's roar, so the monk made a gesture of fright. The hermit laughed aloud. "You old thief!" the monk said.

"What can you do about me?"

The monk gave up.

Later Hsueh Tou said, "This is all right, but these two wicked thieves only knew how to cover their ears to steal the bell."

1. *If you suddenly encounter a tiger, what can you do?*
2. *Why did the hermit laugh?*
3. *"The monk gave up." If you were the monk, what could you do?"*

COMMENTARY: The dog chases the bone, the lion bites people. If you have no mind, everything is yours. If you have mind, you lose everything. If you are cold, use cold medicine. If you are hot, use hot medicine.

353. Un Mun's "Kitchen Pantry and Triple Gate"

Zen Master Un Mun, instructing some monks, said, "Everyone has a light; when you look at it, you don't see it, and it's dark and dim. What is everybody's light?" He himself said, "The kitchen pantry and the triple gate (main gate)." He also said, "Nothing is better than a good thing."

1. *What does "Everyone has a light" mean?*
2. *"When you look at it, you don't see it." What is the meaning of this?*
3. *When it is completely dark, where is your light?*
4. *What is everybody's light?*
5. *"Nothing is better than a good thing." What does that mean?*

COMMENTARY: The Sixth Patriarch said, "Originally nothing." Un Mun said, "Everyone has a light . . ." Light and nothing, are they the same or different? Everyone has two eyes and one mouth.

354. Ji Mun's "Body of Prajna"*

A monk asked Ji Mun, "What is the body of Prajna?"
"An oyster swallowing the bright moon.
"What is the function of Prajna?"
Ji Mun said, "A rabbit getting pregnant."

1. *What is the body of Prajna?*
2. *What does "An oyster swallowing the bright moon" mean?*
3. *What is the function of Prajna?*
4. *"A rabbit getting pregnant." Is that correct or not?*

---

*"Prajna" means wisdom.

COMMENTARY: Truth has no speech or words. True Dharma has no name or form. Where does Prajna come from? What is the function of Prajna? Just do it. When you are tired, sleep. When hungry, eat.

355. Joju's "Three Turning Words"

Zen Master Joju said three turning words to the assembly:

"A mud Buddha cannot cross water; a gold Buddha cannot cross a furnace; a wooden Buddha cannot cross fire."

1. *How does a mud Buddha get to the water?*
2. *How does a gold Buddha get to the furnace?*
3. *How does a wooden Buddha get to the fire?*
4. *Mud Buddha, gold Buddha, wooden Buddha — are they the same or different?*
5. *What kind of Buddha can go anywhere?*

COMMENTARY: The Sixth Patriarch said, "Originally nothing." A sutra says, "Everything is Buddha." Who made Buddha? Who is correct? If you have Buddha, the Buddha will kill you. If you have no Buddha, the Buddha will kill you. What can you do? Go drink tea.

356. Seung Sahn's Four Kinds of "Like This"

Zen Master Seung Sahn said to the assembly, "Our school teaches four kinds of 'like this':
1. 'Without like this' is our true nature, universal substance, primary point, and before-thinking.

2. 'Become one like this' is demonstrating primary point. But primary point has no name, no form, and no speech.
3. 'Only like this' is truth. If you keep primary point, then when you see, when you hear, when you smell, when you taste or touch, all 'like this' is truth.
4. 'Just like this' is just doing, which means correct life from moment to moment. This means always keeping correct situation, correct relationship, and correct function."

1. What is "Without like this?"
2. What is "Become one like this?"
3. What is "Only like this?"
4. What is "Just like this?"

COMMENTARY: This world is complete stillness, so opening or closing your mouth is already a mistake. What can you do? If you keep this mind, you and the universe are never separate. If you hold this mind, you lose your head. One more step is necessary, and then everything is very clear. The sky is blue, the tree is green, the dog is barking, "Woof! Woof!"

How do you function correctly? If someone is hungry, give them food. If someone is thirsty, give them a drink. If you meet the Buddha, bow. If there are ashes on your cigarette, use an ashtray.

357. Seung Sahn's "Subject Just-Like-This, Object Just-Like-This"

Zen Master Seung Sahn said to the assembly, "Our school teaches four kinds of 'like this.' The fourth kind, 'just like this,' has two conditions: subject just-like-this and object just-like-this. 'Subject just-like-this' is subject's correct situation, correct relationship and correct function. 'Object just-like-this' is object's correct situation, correct relationship and correct function."

1. *What is "subject just-like-this?"*
2. *What is "object just-like-this?"*
3. *When all kinds of "like-this" disappear, then what?*

COMMENTARY: An old woman's grandson dies. She can't stop crying. All her relatives and friends try to stop her crying, but they only end up crying with her. Finally, they say, "Let's stop crying and just chant for your grandson." So together they all chant, "Ji Jang Bosal, Ji Jang Bosal . . ."

358. The Sixth Patriarch's Poem

One day Zen Master Seung Sahn said to the assembly, "The Sixth Patriarch's poem hit the head monk's poem."

The head monk's poem says,

Body is Bodhi tree,
Mind is clear mirror's stand.
Always clean, clean, clean.
Don't keep dust.

The Sixth Patriarch's poem says,

Bodhi has no tree,
Clear mirror has no stand.
Originally nothing.
Where is dust?

"With this, the Sixth Patriarch received transmission. But he made a big mistake when he said, 'Originally nothing. Where is dust?' So if you want transmission you must hit the Sixth Patriarch's poem line-by-line."

1. *What is Bodhi?*
2. *What is clear mirror?*
3. *What is "originally nothing?"*
4. *How do you hit the Sixth Patriarch's poem line by line?*

COMMENTARY: If you finish these questions, you become the Buddha's teacher.

359. The Sixth Patriarch's Head

Once, Zen Master Seung Sahn visited the temple of the Sixth Patriarch, Nan Hua Temple on Chogye Mountain in China. Seung Sahn asked the abbot, "Venerable Sir, in Korea there is a temple called San Gye Sah where there is another relic head of the Sixth Patriarch. Now, I see the Patriarch's head is here, too. Which is the true head of the Sixth Patriarch?"

"The one here is the true head," the abbot replied.

Seung Sahn said, "Your head is as white as snow."

"Really?" The abbot touched his head and laughed.

1. *Who is the Sixth Patriarch?*
2. *Which is the true head of the Sixth Patriarch?*
3. *If everything comes from stillness, how did the Sixth Patriarch's head appear?*

COMMENTARY: The Diamond Sutra says, "All formations are appearing and disappearing. If you view all appearing as not appearing, then you can see your original face." Which one is the Sixth Patriarch's original face? Is it Korean or Chinese? If you put it all down, you can see the Sixth Patriarch's original face everywhere. The cucumber is green, the pepper is red.

360. Seung Sahn's "True Buddha"

After being toured through Fu Yuan Temple in China, Zen Master Seung Sahn said to the abbot, Zen Master Chuan Yin, "This temple is filled with big Buddhas and little Buddhas.

221

Which one is the true Buddha?"

Abbot Chuan Yin answered by writing, "Where there is no Buddha, you should pass through rapidly. Where there is a Buddha, you should not stop and stay."

Seung Sahn replied, "I am not asking whether there is a Buddha or not. Please tell me, where is the true Buddha?"

The abbot hesitated.

Seung Sahn said, "The true Buddha is sitting right now on the chair in front of me."

1. *Fu Yuan Temple is filled with big Buddhas and little Buddhas. Which is the true Buddha?*
2. *Abbot Chuan Yin said, "Where there is no Buddha, you should not stop and stay." What does this mean?*
3. *What is the difference between "where there is no Buddha" and "where there is a Buddha"?*

COMMENTARY: Buddha is mind, mind is Buddha. No mind, no Buddha. KATZ! Hit! One finger, dry shit on a stick, three pounds of flax – which is the correct Buddha? If you find the correct Buddha, you get thirty blows. If you cannot find the correct Buddha, you also get thirty blows. What can you do? If you don't understand, go drink tea.

361. Where Is Bodhidharma?

During a recent trip to China, Zen Master Seung Sahn visited Shaolin [K: Sorim] Temple, where Bodhidharma lived. The Master of the temple came out and told the following story about Bodhidharma:

Three years after Bodhidharma died, a Chinese emissary named Song Woon met him on a mountain field. Bodhidharma was barefoot and carrying a long stick with one straw sandal hanging from it. They greeted one another happily and then Bodhidharma went on to India, while Song Woon returned to China. When Song Woon spoke of his meeting with Bodhidharma, he was told that Bodhidharma had been dead for three years. Everyone went to check the stone coffin in which Bodhidharma had been buried. They opened it up and found only one shoe and no body.

Zen Master Seung Sahn asked the Master, "Then Bodhidharma should still be alive. Where is he now?"

The Master just scratched his head.

Seung Sahn answered, "The green pine tree in front of the Buddha Hall."

1. *How did Bodhidharma come back to life?*
2. *Why did Bodhidharma leave one shoe in the coffin?*
3. *Is Bodhidharma alive or dead?*
4. *"The green pine tree in front of the Buddha Hall." What does this mean?*

COMMENTARY: Bodhidharma sat in Sorim for nine years. He didn't understand himself, but he understood this "don't know." This "don't know" has been our great teacher for fifteen hundred years. Three years after he died, Bodhidharma was alive again. If you don't understand, only keep "don't know," and then Bodhidharma will appear in front of you. The mountain is blue, water is flowing.

362. *Seung Sahn's "Dropping Ashes on the Buddha"*

A man came into the Zen Center smoking a cigarette, blowing smoke in the Buddha-statue's face and dropping ashes on its lap. The abbot came in, saw the man, and said, "Are you crazy? Why are you dropping ashes on the Buddha?"

The man answered, "Buddha is everything. Why not?"

The abbot couldn't answer and went away.

1. *"Buddha is everything." What does that mean?*
2. *Why did the man drop ashes on the Buddha?*
3. *If you had been the abbot, how could you have fixed this man's mind?*

COMMENTARY: How do you meet the Buddha? Where do you throw away ashes? It's all very clear. Your correct function is always in front of you.

363. Ko Bong's "Mouse Eats Cat Food"

Seung Sahn visited his teacher, Zen Master Ko Bong, who asked him many difficult kong-ans which Seung Sahn answered easily. After many exchanges, Ko Bong said, "All right, one last question. The mouse eats cat food, but the cat bowl is broken. What does this mean?"

Seung Sahn gave many answers, but to each Ko Bong only said, "No." Seung Sahn became angry and frustrated, completely stuck. After staring into Ko Bong's eyes for fifty minutes, his mind broke open like lightning striking.

1. What is "kong-an?"
2. What is "completely stuck?"
3. What did Seung Sahn attain?

COMMENTARY: Mouse eats cat food, cat bowl is broken, then what? A quarter is twenty-five cents, twenty-five cents buys ice cream; ice cream into the stomach, very good feeling. Ah, wonderful!

364. Seung Sahn's "Three Men Walking"

Three men are walking. The first man makes a sword sound, the second man waves his hands, and the third man picks up a handkerchief.

1. *If you were there, what would be your correct function?*
2. *What is the relationship?*
3. *What is the situation?*

COMMENTARY: The function is all different, but the situation is the same.

365. Seung Sahn's "The 10,000 Dharmas Return to the One"

One day Zen Master Seung Sahn said to the assembly:

"The ten thousand Dharmas return to the One:
Where does the One return to?
Not mind, not Buddha.
Then what?"

Next he said:

"The ten thousand Dharmas return to the One:
Where does the One return to?
It is not one, not zero.
Then what?

"If anyone at this moment can pass these two gates, I will give them *inga*."

1. *What is Dharma?*
2. *Where does the One return to?*
3. *What is the answer to the first gate?*
4. *What is the answer to the second gate?*

COMMENTARY: Don't check – moment to moment just do it.

直進

The Story of Seung Sahn Soen-sa

Seung Sahn Soen-sa was born in 1927 in Seun Choen, North Korea. His parents were Protestant Christians.

Korea at this time was under severe Japanese military rule, and all political and cultural freedom was brutally suppressed. In 1944, Soen-sa joined the underground Korean independence movement. Within a few months he was caught by the Japanese police and narrowly escaped a death sentence. After his release from prison, he and two friends stole several thousand dollars from their parents and crossed the heavily-patrolled Manchurian border in an unsuccessful attempt to join the Free Korean Army.

In the years following World War II, while he was studying Western philosophy at Dong Guk University, the political situation in South Korea grew more and more chaotic. One day Soen-sa decided that he wouldn't be able to help people through his political activities or his academic studies. So he shaved his head and went into the mountains, vowing never to return until he had attained the absolute truth.

For three months he studied the Confucian scriptures, but he was unsatisfied by them. Then a friend of his, who was a monk in a small mountain temple, gave him the Diamond Sutra, and he first encountered Buddhism. "All things that appear in this world are transient. If you view all things that appear as never having appeared, then you will realize your true self." When he read these words, his mind became clear. For the next few weeks he read many sutras. Finally, he decided to become a Buddhist monk and was ordained in October, 1948.

Soen-sa had already understood the sutras. He realized that the only important thing now was practice. So ten days after his ordination, he went further up into the mountains and began a one-hundred-day retreat on Won Gak Mountain (the Mountain of Perfect Enlightenment). He ate only pine-needles, dried and beaten into a powder. For twenty hours every day he chanted the Great Dharani of Original Mind Energy. Several times a day he took ice-cold baths. It was a very rigorous practice.

Soon he was assailed by doubts. Why was this retreat necessary? Why did he have to go to extremes? Couldn't he go down to a small temple in a quiet valley, get married like a Japanese monk, and attain enlightenment gradually, in the midst of a happy family? One night these thoughts became so powerful that he decided to leave and packed his belongings. But the next morning his mind was clearer, and he unpacked. A few days later the same thing happened. And in the following weeks, he packed and unpacked nine times.

By now fifty days had passed, and Soen-sa's body was very exhausted. Every night he had terrifying visions. Demons would appear out of the dark and make obscene gestures at him. Ghouls would sneak up behind him and wrap their cold fingers around his neck. Enormous beetles would gnaw his legs. Tigers and dragons would stand in front of him, bellowing. He was in constant terror.

After a month of this, the visions turned into visions of delight. Sometimes Buddha would come and teach him a sutra. Sometimes Bodhisattvas would appear in gorgeous clothing and tell him that he would go to heaven. Sometimes he would keel over from exhaustion and Kwanseum Bosal would gently wake him up. By the end of eighty days, his body was strong. His flesh had turned green from the pine-needles.

One day, a week before the retreat was to finish, Soen-sa was walking outside, chanting and keeping rhythm with his *moktak*. Suddenly, two boys, eleven or twelve years old, appeared on either side of him and bowed. They were wearing many-colored robes, and their faces were of an unearthly beauty. Soen-sa was very surprised. His mind felt powerful and perfectly clear, so how could these demons have materialized? He walked ahead on the narrow mountain path, and the two boys followed him, walking right through the boulders on either side of the path. They walked together in silence for a half-hour, then, back at the altar, when Soen-sa got up from his bow, they were gone. This happened every day for a week.

Finally it was the hundredth day. Soen-sa was outside chanting and hitting the *moktak*. All at once his body disappeared, and he was in infinite space. From far away he could hear the *moktak* beating, and the sound of his own voice. He remained in this state for some time. When he returned to his body, he understood. The rocks, the river, everything he could see, everything he could hear, all this was his true self. All things are exactly as they are. The truth is just like this.

Soen-sa slept very well that night. When he woke up the next morning, he saw a man walking up the mountain, then some crows flying out of a tree. He wrote the following poem:

> The road at the bottom of Won Gak Mountain
> is not the present road.
> The man climbing with his backpack
> is not a man of the past.
> Tok, tok, tok – his footsteps
> transfix past and present.
> Crows out of a tree.
> Caw, caw, caw.

Soon after he came down from the mountain, he met Zen Master Ko Bong, whose teacher had been Zen Master Man Gong. Ko Bong was reputed to be the most brilliant Zen Master in Korea, and one of the most severe. At this time he was teaching only laymen; monks, he said, were not ardent enough to be good Zen students. Soen-sa wanted to test his enlightenment with Ko Bong, so he went to him with a *moktak* and said, "What is this?" Ko Bong took the *moktak* and hit it. This was just what Soen-sa had expected him to do.

Soen-sa then said, "How should I practice Zen?"

Ko Bong said, "A monk once asked Zen Master Jo-ju, 'Why did Bodhidharma come to China?' Jo-ju answered, 'The pine tree in the front garden.' What does this mean?"

Soen-sa understood, but he didn't know how to answer. He said, "I don't know."

Ko Bong said, "Only keep this don't-know mind. That is true Zen practice."

That spring and summer, Soen-sa did mostly working Zen. In the fall, he sat for a hundred-day meditation session at Su Dok Sa monastery, where he learned Zen language and Dharma-combat. By the winter, he began to feel that the monks weren't practicing hard enough, so he decided to give them some help. One night, as he was on guard-duty (there had been some burglaries), he took all the pots and pans out of the kitchen and arranged them in a circle in the front yard. The next night, he turned the Buddha on the main altar toward the wall and took the incense-burner, which was a national treasure, and hung it on a persimmon tree in the garden. By the second morning the whole monastery was in an uproar. Rumours were flying around about lunatic burglars, or gods coming from the mountain to warn the monks to practice harder.

The third night, Soen-sa went to the nuns' quarters, took seventy pairs of nuns' shoes and put them in front of Zen Master Dok Sahn's room, displayed as in a shoe store. But this time, a nun woke up to go to the outhouse and, missing her shoes, she woke up everyone in the nuns' quarters. Soen-sa was caught. The next day he was brought to trial. Since most of the monks voted to give him another chance (the nuns were unanimously against him), he wasn't expelled from the monastery. But he had to offer formal apologies to all the high monks.

First he went to Dok Sahn and bowed. Dok Sahn said, "Keep up the good work."

Then he went to the head nun. She said, "You've made a great deal too much commotion in this monastery, young man." Soen-sa laughed and said, "The whole world is already full of commotion. What can you do?" She couldn't answer.

Next was Zen Master Chun Song, who was famous for his wild actions and obscene language. Soen-sa bowed to him and said, "I killed all the Buddhas of past, present, and future. What can you do?"

Chun Song said, "Aha!" and looked deeply into Soen-sa's eyes. Then he said, "What did you see?"

Soen-sa said, "You already understand."

Chun Song said, "Is that all?"

Soen-sa said, "There's a cuckoo singing in the tree outside the window."

Chun Song laughed and said, "Aha!" He asked several more questions, which Soen-sa answered without difficulty. Finally, Chun Song leaped up and danced around Soen-sa, shouting, "You are enlightened! You are enlightened!" The news spread quickly, and people began to understand the events of the preceding days.

On January 15, the session was over, and Soen-sa left to see Ko Bong. On the way to Seoul, he had interviews with Zen Master Keum Bong and Zen Master Keum Oh. Both gave him *inga*, the seal of validation of a Zen student's great awakening.

Soen-sa arrived at Ko Bong's temple dressed in his old patched retreat clothes and carrying a knapsack. He bowed to Ko Bong and said, "All the Buddhas turned out to be a bunch of corpses. How about a funeral service?"

Ko Bong said, "Prove it!"

Soen-sa reached into his knapsack and took out a dried cuttlefish and a bottle of wine. "Here are the leftovers from the funeral party."

Ko Bong said, "Then pour me some wine."

Soen-sa said, "Okay. Give me your glass."

Ko Bong held out his palm.

Soen-sa slapped it with the bottle and said, "That's not a glass, it's your hand!" Then he put the bottle on the floor.

Ko Bong laughed and said, "Not bad. You're almost done. But I have a few questions for you." He proceeded to ask Soen-sa the most difficult of the seventeen-hundred traditional Zen kong-ans. Soen-sa answered without hindrance.

Then Ko Bong said, "All right, one last question. The mouse eats cat-food, but the cat-bowl is broken. What does this mean?"

Soen-sa said, "The sky is blue, the grass is green."

Ko Bong shook his head and said, "No."

Soen-sa was taken aback. He had never missed a Zen question before. His face began to grow red as he gave one "like this" answer after another. Ko Bong kept shaking his head. Finally Soen-sa exploded with anger and frustration. "Three Zen Masters have given me *inga*! Why do you say I'm wrong?"

Ko Bong said, "What does it mean? Tell me."

For the next fifty minutes, Ko Bong and Soen-sa sat facing each other, hunched like two tomcats. The silence was electric. Then, all of a sudden, Soen-sa had the answer. It was "just like this."

When Ko Bong heard it, his eyes grew moist and his face filled with joy. He embraced Soen-sa and said, "You are the flower; I am the bee."

On January 25, 1949, Soen-sa received from Ko Bong the Transmission of Dharma, thus becoming the Seventy-Eighth Patriarch in this line of succession. It was the only Transmission that Ko Bong ever gave.

After the ceremony, Ko Bong said to Soen-sa, "For the next three years you must keep silent. You are a free man. We will meet again in five hundred years."

Soen-sa was now a Zen Master. He was twenty-two years old.

STEPHEN MITCHELL

Zen Teaching, Kong-an Practice

Kong-an means public case, or public document. Many years ago in China, whenever government documents were copied, a *chop* or seal was imprinted on the copy so that half of the seal remained on the original document and half on the copy. In order to verify that the copy was authentic, the two halves of the seal were matched. In the Zen tradition, kong-ans are used the same way: the student's understanding of a question is one half and matches the teacher's understanding, which is the other half. When the student and the teacher share the same understanding, it is called "transmission from mind to mind."

Originally, there was no kong-an practice. The Buddha was born and attained enlightenment. He taught his students that everything is impermanent, that desire, anger, and ignorance create suffering; he also taught how to attain freedom from suffering, or *Nirvana*. There were no writings and not much discussion, only meditation practice. After the Buddha died, his disciples had four meetings to write down what he had taught. These writings, called *sutras*, were not written by the Buddha, just as the Gospel was not written by Jesus. They are the words of the disciples. In the years that followed, the disciples debated about what the Buddha actually taught: "The Buddha taught this, the Buddha taught that. . . ." Studying Buddhism became more important than practicing. Also, sects within Buddhism argued with each other.

Then, about fifteen-hundred years ago, Bodhidharma began teaching. He traveled from India to China, where Buddhism had already arrived some three hundred years before. Bodhidharma saw that the people were only using Buddhism to pray for the things they wanted, so he began to teach them correctly. There is a famous story about his first visit to the Emperor Wu of Liang in Southern China, who told Bodhidharma that he had built countless temples, copied countless sutras, and given supplies to countless monks. Then he asked Bodhidharma:

"How much merit have I made?"

"No merit at all."

The Emperor then asked, "What is the highest meaning of the holy truths?"

"No holiness is clear like space."

The Emperor was completely baffled. "Who is facing me?" he asked.

Bodhidharma answered, "Don't know."

Then Bodhidharma went to northern China, where there were many famous temples, but he avoided them all, and sat in a cave near Sorim [Ch: Shaolin], facing the wall. After nine years, a man named Hui Ko came to him in his cave and said:

"Please teach me what Dharma is."

"Bodhidharma replied, "Even if I told you, you would not believe me."

Then Hui Ko cut off his own arm to demonstrate his sincerity. "Oh Master, the pain is terrible! My mind is in awful pain! Please put my mind at rest."

"Give me your mind and I will put it at rest."

"I cannot find it."

Bodhidharma replied, "I have already put your mind at rest."

Upon hearing this, Hui Ko attained enlightenment, and became the Second Patriarch. This was the first Zen teaching: transmission from mind to mind.

The next major change in Zen teaching came with the Sixth Patriarch, who taught, "If you don't make the cause, you have no effect, so don't make anything." He became well-known for this very simple kind of teaching. Once, two monks were watching a flag flapping in the wind. They argued over which was moving, the flag or the wind. Overhearing them, the Sixth Patriarch said, "Neither the flag nor the wind is moving. It is your mind that is moving."

So this new question – "What is mind?" – became an inspiration for Zen monks. Many questions came out of stories such as these: What is life? What is death? What is mind? All of these questions became kong-ans and people started to use them in their own practice. When a student came to him, the Sixth Patriarch asked him,

"Where are you coming from? What kind of thing comes here?"
"Don't know," the student replied.

This is where the "What am I?" kong-an originated. It was the same question that the Buddha practiced with for six years. The Buddha, Bodhidharma, and the Sixth Patriarch all had the same question, "What am I?" and all answered "Don't know." This was the original kong-an practice.

Later, many schools evolved and naturally a variety of techniques grew up within each school. A country boy once asked the Eighth Patriarch, Ma Jo, "What is Buddha?" Ma Jo answered, "Mind is Buddha, Buddha is mind." Later he answered the same boy's question with "No mind, no Buddha." Whereas before the teaching had been simple, now there were many intellectual styles of teaching, and so a kind of word-fighting, or "dharma combat," also appeared. Thus we have *The Blue Cliff Record* and the *Mumon Kwan*, two famous collections of Zen kong-ans.

Zen began to look more cryptic to ordinary people. The practice of Zen and people's everyday lives grew further apart. People couldn't understand esoteric sayings like, "The wooden chicken cries, the stone tiger flies in the sky," or "Do you see the rabbit's horn?" Zen became a practice only for the elite. One always had to look for the hidden meaning, because the words themselves didn't make any sense. This style went on for a while, until more direct teaching returned. "What is Buddhism?" was answered with "Spring comes, the grass grows by itself." So although Zen had developed many kinds of answers to these fundamental questions, all along they were pointing to the truth.

In the past, monks and nuns spent their entire lives in the mountains only practicing Zen. Attaining truth was enough. The correct function of truth was not necessary because they had no connecton to society. But most people today have busy lives with families and jobs – so connecting Zen and everyday life becomes very important. In order to attain your true self, a correct life is necessary. Put it all down, don't make anything and moment to moment keep correct situation, correct relationship, and correct function. Just *do* it. If you practice this, you already attain your true self. But you don't believe that, so you must keep trying. Then correct attainment and correct function happen at the same time. This is a kind of Zen revolution.

In the past, kong-an practicing meant checking someone's enlightenment. Now, we use kong-ans to make our lives correct. This is different from the traditional way of using kong-ans that we talked about earlier. Whether the answers are correct or not doesn't matter – only how can you *use* kong-ans in your everyday life.

Kwan um means "perceive sound." This means perceive your true self. At the same time, perceiving world sound means perceiving that many, many beings are suffering. If you can hear this sound of suffering, then helping is both possible and necessary. That is the Bodhisattva Way. Helping other beings is our practice *and* our job. Correct practicing is not only attaining enlightenment – it's finding enlightenment's *job*. So kong-ans are only a technique to teach you how to do that. Don't be attached to correct answers or incorrect answers. You must use kong-ans to take away your opinions. When you take away your opinions, your mind is clear like space, which means from moment to moment you can reflect any situation and respond correctly and meticulously.

Some people ask, "What is the the best way to work on kong-ans?" An eminent teacher once said, "The ten thousand questions are all one question." Practicing with one question means only go straight, don't know. Just *do* it. If you are attached to a kong-an, you will have a big problem; it's a kind of Zen "sickness." A kong-an is only a finger pointing at the moon. If you are attached to the finger, you cannot perceive the moon. The most important thing is your direction. This direction is Don't Know.

The old style of practice was to go into the mountains, cut off the outside world and just work on one kong-an, sometimes for many years. Our style of practice is learning how to function correctly in everyday life through kong-an practice. So, when you are doing something, just do it. When you just do it, there is no thinking – no subject and no object. Inside and outside become one. This is correct kong-an practice - only doing it. Moment to moment everyday life is our kong-an. Our Zen revolution.

Index

242